Why People Disagree

(and Get Used)

Steven Arnold

Copyright © Steven Arnold 2024

All rights reserved.

ISBN: 978-1-7360471-1-8

Fir Valley Publishing

*Those with power fear most
those who think for themselves*

Contents

Introduction 6

I. The Thing About Opinions 9
A Conceptual Framework 10
Deconstructing Opinions 17
Why It Matters 25
Case Study: Listening 30
Case Study: The Economy 36
Case Study: Crime 42

II. Why People Disagree 51
Applying the Framework 52
Diagnosing Disagreements 57
Resolving Disagreements - Formal Methods 65
Winning Arguments vs Changing Minds 70
Living with Unresolved Disagreements 74
Case Study: Disdain 77
Case Study: The Federal Budget 81
Case Study: Social Security 91

III. How People Get Used 101
Applying the Framework 102
Power 104
Influence 109

Manipulation	113
Subjugation	117
Case Study: Outrage	121
Case Study: Health Care	126
Case Study: The American Dream	131
IV. What is to be Done?	137
Leverage the Framework	138
Define the Problem and Why You Care	142
Know Why You Have a Right to Succeed	145
Focus on Key Leverage Points to Target	149
Choose the Tools and Methods to Use	154
Start	160
Case Study: Trust	165
Case Study: Occupy Mars	171

Introduction

Despite its cover, you are reading this book! Let's see if it will be worthwhile.

The intent is to lay out a framework for understanding what an opinion is, then walk through how disagreements are a result of conflicting beliefs that support opinions. It may seem like a stretch, but the same framework explains how people get used - when our beliefs about our world and ourselves are manipulated.

You might wonder if such content is theoretical. Don't worry. We will not get into the philosophical weeds of reality, truth, or knowledge. This book is practical because it will help you think for yourself - which leads to a kind of freedom we don't experience often enough. You will learn when to walk away from unproductive debates. You will recognize how people get used and what you can do about it.

This book has four parts that tackle, in turn, opinions, disagreements, getting used, and what to do. Look over the table of contents to get a sense of the scope.

Be careful. This book is quite dense. Like a sheet of peanut brittle, it is not to be consumed in one sitting. Skim the first few chapters, then feel free to bounce around.

The case studies deep-dive into selected topics. The analysis in the case studies is not meant to be definitive. On the contrary, the cases are intended to demonstrate how ordinary people can look at easily-available data and form their own opinions.

When you look at a data table in a case study, turn away from your phone and computer. Spend up to 30 seconds focused on the information. Come up with at least one insight on your own. You'll find that your insights are as valid as anyone else's.

Thinking for yourself is hard work. It is one of those things that we *should* do, but may not get around to (like exercising, meditating, or decluttering). The key to thinking for yourself is to find a balance between having the strength of your own convictions to hold on to your beliefs and being open-minded – willing to challenge your beliefs.

Take hope. After you finish this book, you should feel confident in your ability to choose good thought-leaders (people you trust to do your thinking for you). You should also feel confident that you can deconstruct on the fly a disagreement or attempts to manipulate you.

Give yourself a chance. You will find this book powerful and worthwhile.

I. The Thing About Opinions

Where we explore the nature of opinions. We propose a framework for deconstructing an opinion into a primary-belief justified by a collection of supporting beliefs. This framework makes opinions easier to understand. Most people appreciate being understood before their opinions are challenged.

A Conceptual Framework

Children are asked a lot of (at times rude) questions:
"How old are you?"
"What do you want to be when you grow up?"
"What's your favorite color?"
"Who would win in a fight - Batman or Superman?"

Each of these questions gets at a "belief." As children get older, they accumulate beliefs so that they can have proper "opinions" like grownups.

Adults are full of beliefs and opinions

Part of the burden of growing up is the expectation that we must have a point of view about many things. Even when we know next to nothing, we ought to have something to say.

Topic	Opinions expected of us
Personal	School and career choices
	Where to live
	How to start and stop romantic relationships
	What does my car say about me?
Work	How to do my job
	How to get promoted
	Is my boss asking me to do something unethical?
Voting	School bonds

Topic	Opinions expected of us
	US President
	5th Grade Class President (deep down you know you could have won)
Economy	Why GDP, tax law, and the federal funds rate matter
	What makes stock prices go up and down
Policy	Gun control
	Abortion
	Defense spending
	Am I red, blue, or purple?
Religion	Does God exist?
	What heaven is like
	Why my religion is the best
	When is killing OK?

So, what is an "opinion"?

All opinions are beliefs, but not all beliefs are opinions. An "opinion" is a special kind of belief-statement that makes an assertion. Opinions can be:

- Descriptive - how things *are* (or have been) and why.
- Predictive - how things *will be* in the future under certain conditions.
- Prescriptive - how things *should be* given norms and rules to follow.

So, what is *not* an "opinion"?

Of the questions above that a child must answer, only one is an opinion. Who would win in a superhero fight is an opinion that requires some careful analysis. How old you are is a fact, not an opinion. Your favorite color and career goals are personal preferences, not opinions. Let's further explore some types of beliefs that are not opinions.

Matters of fact beliefs - descriptive statements that do not include an explanation of "why" things are the way they are. "The population of our town has declined more than ten percent" is a descriptive factual belief. That belief can be challenged with alternative data, but it is not an opinion. To say, "Our town's population decline is due to a lack of good jobs" is a descriptive statement with some logic of cause and effect meant to explain a fact. It's an opinion.

Personal preference beliefs - For example, "I like ketchup more than mustard" is a belief. Preference beliefs are hard to argue. Your favorite color or condiment is what it is. If instead, someone says, "I like ketchup more than mustard, because ketchup is healthier," then we have a logic-based opinion that can be disputed.

Diagnosis beliefs - A doctor's diagnosis is a belief, not an opinion. A diagnosis is based on symptoms, tests, and professional guidelines. When the conversation with a doctor shifts to prognosis and treatment options, then you have "opinions" that take into account risks, uncertainty, and quality of life for the patient.

What we do when we must defend an opinion

All this talk of beliefs and opinions, what is the point? It boils down to how we explain our opinions to people. An opinion-belief is supported by a collection of beliefs.

You might share your opinions all day, but at times you will be challenged to justify an opinion. People might say to you, "Why do you think that?" "Prove it," or "You're crazy!" To justify an opinion, you must explain yourself with some supporting-beliefs along the lines of who, what, when, where, why, and how.

An example of justifying/ defending an opinion
(Something you might overhear while getting coffee.)

He said, "Poverty causes crime."

She said, "How do you know that?"

He said, "I saw a chart online. It was a map that showed poverty rates and crime rates by neighborhood. High poverty areas have high crime."

She said, "OK. Good data. But correlation does not prove causation. Does poverty cause crime? Does crime cause poverty? Does something else cause both?"

He said, "I don't know."

She said, "Who wrote the article with the chart?"

He said, "A guy who works for a foundation that supports eradicating poverty."

It is a lot to expect people in everyday life to have coherent, well-organized responses when their opinions are challenged unexpectedly. So, belief-statements intended to justify an opinion may randomly pour out. They may not make any sense. They may be unconvincing.

Often, when challenged about their opinions, people will cite a trusted source (Wikipedia, cable news) or an authority (the IRS, popular social media influencer). For people who haven't given much thought to their opinions, hearsay is about the best they can do to justify their opinions.

A Defining Framework

Everyone has an assortment of opinions and supporting beliefs. A churning tumbling jumble. When your mind is called upon to defend an opinion, it casts a net into your sea of beliefs and hauls up what it hopes will be enough to justify the opinion. For experienced communicators, opinions and supporting evidence will flow seamlessly, logically. For the rest of us, it is a mess.

The following Opinion-Framework format can help give some structure to understanding someone's opinions. When listening to an opinion and its supporting beliefs, try to pinpoint the opinion then sort the rest of the beliefs you hear into three categories:

OPINION - belief about how things are, have been, will be, or should be. Opinions usually involve some level of uncertainty. Try to reduce an opinion-belief to a concise statement.

DATA - what the opinion-holder believes (or claims) are accepted, objective facts and data.

MODELS - opinion-holder's mental models, theories, and cause-and-effect logic for how things work.

VALUES - core beliefs that drive subjective choices and explain why people have certain preferences.

Let's see how to use this Framework. Imagine you are getting coffee (again), and you listen-in to how a teenager tries to convince her parent that she needs a new, rather than used, car.

You jot down the key points, adding an initial (D, M, or V) for data, model, value. (Note, X means unassigned, since not all statements in a discussion are relevant. This teenager is tossing every reason she can think of.)

Here is what you heard:
- Need all-wheel drive for the snow (M)
- A dumpy, old car is embarrassing (V)
- Need a reliable car when running errands for the family and driving younger siblings and their friends to activities (M)
- A new audio system will help get better grades in orchestra class (M)
- Promise not to drink and drive (D)
- A new car is safer, and bigger is better (D, V)
- I'm a better driver than my friends are, and having a bigger, better car means I would not be riding in their cars (M?)
- You never listen to me (X)
- I never get to do what I want (X)
- A new car is more reliable and has lower maintenance costs (D)
- I can get a part time job to help pay for it (D?)

Beliefs versus Truths

"Beliefs" and "Models" seem like soft words to use in our lofty conceptual framework. Why aren't we saying that opinions are supported by "absolutes" like facts and data and logic?

We may make a statement that we consider to be unassailable truth. We might be shocked that anyone could disagree. However, if we refuse to question our own fundamental beliefs, then we will falter as we navigate disagreements and counter getting used – expecting everyone else to see the light and change.

So, when we are in a good faith debate or negotiation, we should be open-minded. Likewise, if we are dealing with people who use power or lies to get their way, we need to let go of the notion that truth has an impact. Softer words ("beliefs" and "models") give us the flexibility we need to live in the real world.

Key points:
- We are full of beliefs that tumble in our minds
- Opinions are a special kind of belief about why things are or how things should be
- We justify, or explain, our opinion-beliefs by snatching and sharing a set of supporting-beliefs we cull from the tumbling rabble of beliefs in our minds
- The Opinion-Framework is very effective at making sense of an opinion and its supporting-beliefs by separating the supporting-beliefs into data, models, and values

Deconstructing Opinions

OK. The previous chapter was necessary but pedantic and difficult to follow. Glad that's over!

It's easier to put into practice the Opinion-Framework by deconstructing a prepared speech, as opposed to off-the-cuff remarks. We will tackle three historical examples (two speeches and one interview) to illustrate how to represent an opinion and supporting belief-statements.

Note how, in a prepared speech, the speaker has control of the narrative. In an interview, the two persons involved may tussle for control of the narrative.

Eisenhower and the military-industrial complex

Historically, the US had a peacetime economy that would be jolted by a declaration of war into producing military weapons and equipment. An on-off cycle. During the Cold War, government leaders recognized that defense spending needed to operate in peace and at war at a steady pace.

In his Farewell Address (January 1961), President Eisenhower is famous for warning Americans about the risks of a powerful military-industrial complex that would be needed to provide constant readiness. Eisenhower worried that military-driven foreign policy and R&D might skew diplomacy and reduce our efforts to help other nations pursue freedom and a better life for their citizens.

Reading his speech, today, one might be surprised at its scope. Compared to present-day partisan rhetoric, Eisenhower's remarks may seem quaint, but his tone is refreshing and inspiring. He gives as much airtime to American ideals, our role as global leaders in a democracy facing totalitarian regimes, and sustainable environmentalism as he does to worrying about the military-industrial complex. As it turned out, the complex he warned of has diminished: defense spending as a percent of GDP has decreased, universities have reduced dependence on government-funded research (an outcome of the Vietnam War), and tech companies have access to a lot of private wealth for independent research.

Let's see what we can extract from Ike's speech:
OPINION beliefs
America's purpose is to keep the peace, support human progress, and "enhance liberty, dignity, and integrity among people and among nations."

That purpose is threatened by the Cold War and "hostile ideology."

DATA supporting-beliefs
"America is today the strongest ... and most productive nation in the world."

"We face a hostile ideology - global ... atheistic ... ruthless ... and insidious."

We think that fixing the latest crisis is a cure-all.

There has been a technological revolution. Funding for research has been increasingly paid for by the Federal government.

Powerful countries can make unilateral decisions that impact smaller countries.

It is tempting to use natural resources to live for today and not worry about tomorrow.

MODELS supporting-beliefs
"America's leadership and prestige depend ... on how we use our power in the interests of world peace and human betterment."

Policy needs to evolve from crisis response to balanced long-term initiatives.

Research is essential to technology development.

Powerful countries must allow other countries a seat at the table as equals.

Our current geopolitical situation requires that we have a permanent military armaments industry and perpetual readiness of our armed forces.

We must limit military-industrial complex influence on policy and scientific research.

We must be stewards of the earth's resources.

VALUES supporting-beliefs
　　Peace
　　Human betterment
　　Strength/ Resolve
　　Humility
　　Opportunity/ Freedom

Martin Luther King, Jr. and the Dream

The 1963 March on Washington for Jobs and Freedom was a massive logistical and political undertaking. It is remembered for one speech that did not go according to plan.

The march was planned for months by a group of civil rights activists (notably A. Philip Randolph and Bayard Rustin). Eighteen speakers and performers were on the program for the event at the Lincoln Memorial. The organizers expected 100,000 attendees. An estimated 250,000 people showed up.

There were several objectives for the march: civil rights legislation, better wages, anti-discrimination, nonviolence, and elimination of Jim Crow laws that enforced segregation.

In previous speeches, King had talked about the "dream," but he and others thought it would be too soft for the protest march.

Mahalia Jackson was King's favorite gospel singer. She was a strong supporter of civil rights. She had performed on prior occasions when King delivered speeches, and she was familiar with the "dream speech." She was seated on the stage with other speakers as King delivered his remarks. Caught up in the moment, during his speech, she shouted, "Talk about the dream, Martin." It is said that King paused, set aside his prepared remarks, and veered off-script into the "I have a dream" that we remember.

If you had been there, here are some notes you might have jotted down on your copy of the program.

Deconstructing Opinions

OPINION belief
There will be a day when we will have full rights of life, liberty and pursuit of happiness; but we should not wait - there is urgency and gradualism is unacceptable

DATA supporting-beliefs
Documents have failed: Declaration of Independence, Constitution, Emancipation Proclamation

Systemic segregation and discrimination persist

African-Americans are subjected to denial of voting rights, police brutality, ghetto conditions and segregation, attacks on dignity and self-esteem, racial injustice

MODELS supporting-beliefs
America's promises have been broken

America is a land of plenty and there is plenty for all to achieve the American Dream

When enough people support Freedom, then change will happen

It will require that people of different races and religion unite and demand freedom for African Americans - black people can't get there on their own

Unrest of 1963 will not subside and go away - demand for change cannot be ignored or placated so as to maintain the status quo

Nonviolence will be more effective than violent actions - people must not give in to hatred and wrongful deeds

VALUES supporting-beliefs
  Equal rights
  Promises must be honored
  Faith in God
  Faith in America and the rule of law

Frost-Nixon and presidential power

In 1977, former President Nixon agreed to be interviewed by David Frost, a British journalist who had a long-running television interview series in America. Nixon had been out of the public eye for two years following his resignation. He was writing his memoir, published in 1978. For Nixon, the interviews were an opportunity for publicity and a chance to shape public perception of him.

Frost financed and syndicated the interviews himself, covering production costs and paying Nixon a hefty fee. The tv and radio broadcasts were a sensation. Frost was well-prepared and not the lightweight interviewer Nixon might have expected.

Both Frost and Nixon faced risks yet had much to gain from the interviews.

Watching this interview, you would have had one of those "Did he say that?" moments. At one point, Nixon says, "Well, when the President does it, that means that it is not illegal." He was referring to a plan drafted by a staffer in the White House Counsel office that included illegal wiretapping, burglary, mail opening, and infiltrating anti-war groups. In July 1970, Nixon approved the plan, but he rescinded that approval after several days.

During the interview, Nixon described the turbulence in America he faced in 1970 and defended his view of the President's authority. After the interview aired, he had to do some damage control.

OPINION

Certain circumstances give President the authority to take actions that are illegal.

But this idea does not suggest that the President is above the law.

DATA

Domestic threats were increasing. Groups were actively disrupting everyday life and trying to overthrow the government and rule of law.

Violence was putting citizens and public order at risk, including hijackings, bomb threats, and violent protests.

Inadequate coordination of the FBI, CIA, and NSA made us more vulnerable to these threats.

Our nation was splitting apart.

Actions of dissident citizens (such as Ellsberg releasing the Pentagon Papers) caused harm.

MODELS

When warranted by national security or domestic tranquility interests, some actions that are unlawful can be carried out by people, at the request of the President, without violating the law.

The President has to use judgement in balancing individual versus national interests. The President can't just run amok.

The President faces elections, congressional oversight, budget negotiations – which are countervailing powers that limit the President's autonomy.

Coordinating law enforcement agencies and judiciously using tools like surveillance and burglary will improve counter-espionage as well as handling domestic groups advocating and using violence.

Keeping the peace at home and keeping support for the war were essential in order to get the enemy to negotiate an honorable end to the Vietnam War.

VALUES
    National security
    Personal security and safety of citizens
    Defending our Constitution

Key points:
- The Opinion-Framework helps organize the supporting-beliefs for an opinion belief
- A strong opinion-argument uses all three layers of support: data, models, and values

Why It Matters

Opinion - Data - Models - Values...

Why is this framework useful?
Listening to an argument, an interview, or a debate can be overwhelming. There are lots of words, that may not be well-organized. It is hard to remember everything that you hear.

The Opinion-Framework offers a simple way to process an opinion and its collection of supporting-beliefs. Sorting a sequence of statements into data, model, and values helps you sense where the support of an opinion seems thin. You may notice that the data and models don't relate to each other. The level of emotion in the speaker's tone and rhetoric can help you identify when value-beliefs are more important.

Strawman versus Steelman
Strawman is an underhanded debate technique. A strawman argument presents an easy-to-refute version of someone's opinion. By knocking down the "straw man" that you propose, you can win the argument. The tricky part is to distract people from noticing that the strawman is flawed or incomplete.

Here are a few examples of strawman techniques:

- Oversimplifying - "He is saying that rent control *alone* will solve homelessness."
- Taking things out of context - "They want big companies to be able to see your tax returns."
- Exaggerating - "They want to give every homeless person free rent in a luxury downtown apartment."

The Opinion-Framework can help you to build a "steelman" argument. Unlike a strawman, a steelman presents a version of someone's opinion that is good enough that that person will concede that the steelman is accurate. Offering a steelman demonstrates that you understand what another person is saying. Once both parties agree on a shared version of a person's argument, then strengths and weaknesses in the steelman can be debated.

Isn't this Framework just the Scientific Method?
No… Well, there *is* some overlap …

The scientific method is a process of theory and discovery meant to understand the natural world or any measurable system. There is an ongoing cycle of observation, hypothesis, prediction, experimentation, and assessment that to some degree supports or refutes a theory

Except for the Values category of the Opinion Framework, there *is* a high overlap with the Scientific Method:

Opinion Framework	Scientific Method
Opinion	Theories
	Predictions

Opinion Framework	Scientific Method
Data	Observations
	Descriptions
	Experimental results
Models	Hypotheses
	Experimental designs
Values	Objectivity
	Skepticism

Using the scientific method means accepting some boundaries and discipline that don't apply when you are defending ordinary opinions. A hypothesis must be falsifiable through objective testing and observation by an unbiased person. There is a high burden of proof. Ideas that challenge prevailing concepts are supposed to be given a fair hearing.

As for values, the scientific method is limited to an unemotional understanding of how things are. How things should be, or how people want things to be, are determined by our core values and emotions and are outside the bounds of the scientific method. You and I may believe in aliens, but scientists do not say that they "believe" in extraterrestrial life. They speak of "likelihoods" based on evidence.

These constraints hamstring science in debates. Opinion-makers do not have to back up their claims with clear cause-and-effect models and experiments that people can perform for themselves. Opinion-makers can speak in absolute terms, while scientists talk of "likelihoods" and "probabilities."

People are messy

Values and emotions are supposed to be absent in the scientific method. Economists often make the simplifying assumption that people are rational when making decisions that involve risk. In the real world, values drive human messiness in opinion-beliefs.

In the Opinion-Framework, supporting beliefs can be categorized into DATA, MODELS, and VALUES. Given enough time, it might be possible to align people's beliefs about data and models being right or wrong. But, aligning someone's beliefs about data and models does not necessarily lead to agreement.

Two people facing the same decision, who have matching beliefs as to data and models, can have differences in how they rank and apply their values that lead to differences of opinion. For example, you and a friend are at a bungee-jumping venue. You both may have the same understanding of the equipment and the risks. However, the two of you may have very different relative weighting for the values of safety and adventure. Only one of you really wants to jump, but you both make the jump. In addition to safety and adventure, there is a third value in play: personal reputation. How we are perceived in the eyes of our peers overcomes our fear for our safety.

The thing about values is that they are not inherently right or wrong. Each person has an assortment of value-beliefs. Depending on the situation, some values are more applicable and weighted more heavily than others in supporting an opinion.

Key points:
- The Opinion-Framework helps build a steelman argument
- The scientific method discipline excludes values-driven beliefs
- Scientists must be open-minded, which makes them seem weak in a debate
- The rest of us get away with opinions based on irrational and emotional beliefs

Case Study: Listening

Effective Listening

In most situations, you are a passive, unresponsive listener. You try to monitor, with as little effort as possible, the overwhelming input from media, news, and bosses. However, there are times when you must be an active listener. When actively listening, you may be supportive or challenging.

So, here are several roles an active listener with good intentions can play:

Supportive roles	Challenging roles
Follower/ Disciple - accept the opinion without question	*Antagonist* - battle to win the debate
Customer - what does the opinion mean for me	*Devil's Advocate* - poke holes in an opinion
Sounding Board - listen without judging	*Arbitrator* - listen then render a decision

Supportive listeners should not accept an opinion without doing some sanity checks. Challenging listeners should have some basis for their critiques of an opinion. Whether you are supporting or challenging, as you listen to an opinion, keep attuned to flaws in the data, models, and values supporting-beliefs that you hear.

DATA-related flaws

When people share facts and data as givens, don't be shy about questioning their validity. We are all prone to cognitive bias and misreading what data is telling us.

Cognitive Bias	Description
Priming	Affected by first impressions
Confirmation	Accept information that is consistent with preconceptions and discredit information that is not consistent
Anchoring	It is difficult to let go of current beliefs and change their opinion
Affinity	Agree with people who are like us
Self-serving	Claim credit for successes more than accept blame for failures
Selection	Sample is not a good representation of the population

Data Interpretation	Description
Extreme Scales	Difficulty in grasping very small and very big numbers
Volatility	Underestimate risk (e.g., volatile stock prices). Assign too much meaning to year-over-year growth and decline rates.
Visual Data	Charts can be manipulated to influence the viewer

Data Interpretation	Description
Correlation versus Causation	Two variables that track each other might be caused by other factors
Probabilities	Medical test results can be difficult to interpret. False positives can be more likely than true positives.

MODELS-related flaws

We often have a poor understanding of how things work. How many of us can troubleshoot, and repair, our car's engine? Financial news analysts are confident about why the market was up last week, but they can't predict next week's results. We want to help people overcome addictions, but there are no easy answers that are 100% effective.

In many circumstances, we are not rational. There is a popular field of study, behavioral economics, that explores how we make choices that are contrary to our best interests. Here are a few behavioral economics principles that apply to flaws in our mental models:

Principle	Description
Cognitive Limits	We can only handle so much information and complexity
Loss Aversion	We treat losses differently from gains
Framing	How a choice is defined has an effect. For example, you can increase participation in a 401k by having people opt out rather than opt in.
Availability Bias	We often make decisions based on data that comes easily to mind or is recent

Principle	Description
	than data that is specifically related to the decision.
Simplistic Rules	Over-simplified mental models (or rules of thumb) can be harmful.

VALUES-related inconsistencies

There are a lot of value-beliefs in our culture:

Category	Example Values
Self	Honesty, Freedom, Life, Kindness, Courage, Honor, Adventure, Safety, Faith, Self-Esteem, Responsibility, Self-Reliance, Competitiveness
Relationships	Fidelity, Trust, Respect, Generosity, Unselfishness, Connectedness, Passion, Belonging, Equality
Work	Integrity, Accountability, Success, Wealth, Power, Fun, Meaning, Loyalty, Balance, Professionalism, Innovation, Creativity
Society	Security, Autonomy, Patriotism, Strength, Fairness, Charity, Justice, Prosperity, Affiliation, Tolerance

All such values are present all the time. However, at any moment, only a handful of them tend to be relevant. Those relevant values are weighted in importance depending on the situation.

For example, people can:
- Be pro-life about pregnancy, but pro death penalty for serial killers
- Support property rights but draw the line at a neighbor painting polka dots on his house
- Favor tax deductions for business vehicles but be against child tax credits
- Be frugal when clipping coupons but pay for premium upgrades on a new car (self-esteem and image can matter more than saving money)

So, a value is not intrinsically right or wrong. How much one value or another supports an opinion depends upon the situation and circumstance. Over time, social norms shape how we rank and apply our values. Society rewards competitiveness with financial success, up to a point. Excess competitiveness is reined in by shame, such as the looks you get when shoving an elderly person aside to get the last doughnut.

The issue isn't whether a value is wrong. What may bother us more is when our values and behaviors seem inconsistent.

Company leaders are often inconsistent in applying values. Talk of work-life balance does not ring true when employees are repeatedly asked to work nights and weekends. Executives may speak of loyalty and pulling for each other, yet they can be the first to seek other opportunities when times get tough.

Mixed messages about values can make a day in the life of a child confusing. Take soccer. The point of the game is to win. Scoring a goal gets the biggest cheers and teaches assertiveness. Passing the ball teaches teamwork and unselfishness. But stopping to help an opponent who tripped and may be hurt shows empathy and makes parents emotional. Adults are hard to figure out.

Key points:
- Active listening is hard work
- Be clear as to your role as a listener. Are you supportive or challenging?
- The Opinion-Framework helps you to listen more effectively - recognizing flaws and inconsistencies in data, models, and values supporting-beliefs

Case Study: The Economy

If you want to complain, the economy has something for everyone. Let's look at some DATA so you can practice thinking for yourself. Put down your phone and take a few minutes develop your own insights.

Snapshot of the Economy

Gross Domestic Product (GDP) represents the US economy. You could spend a year studying the data. However, even a summary data table tells some stories.

Defense spending as a percentage of GDP has declined since 1980. Residential investment's share of GDP dipped in 2010, showing the effects of the housing crisis and the Great Recession. Services have grown, in part due to Health Care.

In 1960, health care (in Services) and Food (in Nondurable goods) were each roughly 5% of total GDP. Since then, Food has remained about 5%. Health care grew from 5% of GDP to roughly 17% currently. We spend three times more on health care than food!

US Gross Domestic Product ($ billions)

	1980	2010	2020
Gross domestic product	$2,857	$15,049	$21,323
Personal expenditures:			
Durable goods	8%	7%	8%
Nondurable goods	20%	15%	14%
Services	33%	46%	45%
Private investment:			
Nonresidential	14%	12%	13%
Residential	5%	3%	4%
Government:			
Federal Defense	6%	6%	4%
Federal Nondefense	3%	3%	3%
State and local	11%	12%	12%
Net exports	0%	-4%	-3%

Source: Bureau of Economic Analysis

Impact on Consumers

How does GDP growth translate to personal spending? It turns out that the proportions of spending by category are fairly stable over the past few decades.

Food and Transportation have declined somewhat. Healthcare, Retirement/ Social Security, and Housing have increased. Wait a minute! Healthcare as a percentage of GDP is up by a factor of three, but consumer spending on healthcare hasn't even doubled. How's that?

Employers and governments pay a lot of health care costs. These benefits don't show up as personal income or spending. Consumers (patients) don't feel in their wallets the full cost of health care. However, employers have been shifting more of the health care premiums and costs to employees.

Consumer Expenditures

	1984	2002	2022
Number of consumer units (000s)	90,223	112,108	134,090
Income before taxes	$23,464	$49,430	$94,003
Income after taxes	$21,237	$46,934	$83,195
Average number in consumer unit	2.6	2.5	2.4
Average Annual Expenditures	$21,975	$40,677	$72,967
Food and Alcohol	16%	14%	14%
Housing	30%	33%	33%
Apparel and Services	6%	4%	3%
Transportation	20%	19%	17%
Healthcare	5%	6%	8%
Entertainment	5%	5%	5%
Other	9%	9%	8%
Retirement Savings Plans	9%	10%	12%

Source: Bureau of Labor Statistics

Employment

Job creation was a miracle of 20th century technology and innovation. After 1900, people shifted toward urban and manufacturing jobs. Family farms faded, replaced with industrial agriculture. Labor productivity increased. The middle class could aspire to owning a home and putting kids through college. After 1960, Services sectors (banking and health care) grew. More women entered the workforce.

Look at the 40-year growth factors. The number of employed-people grew from about half the population to nearly two-thirds. Wages and Salaries, as a percent of GDP, declined. That is good for productivity. The issue is that growth in wages per job lagged GDP growth.

Employment Related Data

	1982	2022	'82 to '22 Growth
US Population (millions)	233	331	1.4X
Jobs (millions)	114	212	1.9X
Jobs % of Population	49%	64%	
GDP ($ trillions)	$3.3	$25.7	7.8X
Wages & Salaries ($ trillions)	$1.5	$10.5	7.0X
Wages % of GDP	45%	41%	
Wages per Job ($000s)	$13.2	$49.5	3.8X

Source: Bureaus of Economic Analysis, Bureau of Labor Statistics, Census Bureau

Poverty

Progress in the war on poverty was made in the 1960's. After 1970, the poverty rate for adults over age 65 continued to improve, likely due to social security. Yet, poverty persists.

Note that poverty rates for children (people under age 18) are higher than for adults. Be careful about your mental MODELS when drawing conclusions from that data. Before you conclude that poor people have more children than the rest of the population, you should think about how poverty is defined. The poverty income level goes up with household size. Children add to household size but don't add to household income.

Math and statistics can be tricky to interpret. Consider a household of two working adults without children whose income is above the poverty line. If they have two children, then they might fall below the poverty line if their income doesn't go up enough. Assume that they then get divorced and split their income. The parent with custody of the kids might then be in a household below the poverty line and the other parent might be in a single person household above the poverty line.

Poverty rates by age group

Year	Under 18	18 to 65	Over 65
1959	27%	17%	35%
1966	18%	11%	29%
1970	15%	9%	25%

Year	Under 18	18 to 65	Over 65
1975	17%	9%	15%
1980	18%	10%	16%
1985	21%	11%	13%
1990	21%	11%	12%
1995	21%	11%	11%
2000	16%	10%	10%
2005	18%	11%	10%
2010	22%	14%	9%
2015	20%	12%	9%
2020	16%	11%	9%

Source: Census Bureau

Key points:
- With a little research, we can gather trustworthy data and support our own opinions about policy issues
- Our economy has generated new jobs but the wages per job have not kept up
- Poverty persists despite the economic miracles of innovation and technology-driven productivity
- These insights raise VALUES questions: Are we better off now than previous generations? Should people serve the economy or vice versa?

Case Study: Crime

Crime threatens our core value of security. Promising to fight crime scores political points. Let's explore crime to test the usefulness of the Opinion-Framework.

This case study is intended to be less than satisfying. Crime policy is multifaceted. So, it is hard to decide what to fix. The data is spotty due to underreporting and inconsistent tracking. There are deeply divisive conflicting values at play. Nevertheless, let's give it a shot.

Pretend that you are at home with nothing to do over a long weekend. In recent weeks, you have learned that a neighbor's car was vandalized, a friend was robbed of his wallet outside of a restaurant, and an elderly relative lost money in an online scam. Crime seems to be creeping closer to home and getting personal. You decide that you want to do something about crime.

Where to start?

You get online. You read lots of articles and blogs. You get something to drink. You listen to a few podcasts. You end up with a scattering of assorted notes.

It isn't neat and tidy. It feels like you have only scratched the surface of this topic. You aren't sure that you will come away with any insights. Regardless, let's sort your jumble of notes into categories:

Data - beliefs that describe how things are across some crime-related topics.

Models – cause-and-effect beliefs that describe different schools of thought about prosecuting and preventing crime.

Values - core beliefs that might push and pull your opinions in surprising directions.

DATA

You listed categories of crime.

Crime Type	Description
Violent	murder, assault, rape, domestic violence and other crimes against persons
Property	theft, burglary, arson
Financial	fraud, bribery, tax evasion, white collar corruption
Vice and Drugs	prostitution, obscenity, illegal drug sales or use
Crimes against the state	spying, treason, insurrection, sedition, damaging public property and infrastructure

You searched for statistics about crime.

You found that there may be some issues with the data. Violent and property crimes have been tracked for years, but data for other crimes is incomplete. Most violent and property crimes are not reported. Most crimes reported to police are not solved. Not all police departments provide data to central registries. Nevertheless, here is some data.

2022 US violent and property crime rates (per 100,000 people)

Crime Category	Rate
All Violent Crimes	377
Homicide	7
Rape	42
Aggravated assault	273
All Property Crimes	1974
Burglary	273
Larceny-theft	1417

Source: FBI Crime Data Explorer

Crime rates are much lower now than hundreds of years ago. For example, homicides are three to five times lower than the 18th century. Since 1900, in general, crime is down, but there have been surges in crime rates (1920's, post-World War Two, and the 1970's to early 1990's).

Since the 1990s, crime rates have generally declined. However, most people believe that crime has increased since the 1990s. With 24-hour news, the internet, and social media newsfeeds - technology and algorithms make if feel like crime is worse now than in the past.

Compared to similar countries, the US has higher crime rates and incarceration rates, and much higher gun ownership rates. The US is the only country with more civilian firearms than people. The US has less than 5% of the world's population and about 20% of the world's prisoners and 40% of the world's guns.

You looked at the cost of the Criminal Justice System
About half of a percent of the US population are prisoners (about 1.2 million people in federal and state facilities). In addition to prisons, more than half a million people at any point in time during 2022 were in local jails (about 80% if them not convicted, but waiting for the wheels of justice to turn). Most people are in jail for a short time, so over the course of that year perhaps five to seven million people may have been in jail.

You might see claims that one in three adult Americans have a criminal record. That doesn't mean much. Having a "record" does not mean you were convicted. But, having a record, especially having been arrested, is a serious handicap when filling out a job application.

The average cost of incarcerating a prisoner is roughly $40,000 per year. About $300 billion is spent directly on criminal justice costs: police, courts, corrections. About three times that amount might be the financial impact of lost earnings, health effects, and other impacts on families of those accused and in prison. So, perhaps $1.2 trillion in total costs.

MODELS
You have uncovered an overwhelming assemblage of cause-and-effect MODELS that may explain the DATA you have collected.

What causes criminals to commit crimes?
Nearly all of us might act impulsively in a crisis in a way that hurts someone. Hard to predict crimes of passion. If we want to reduce crime, we should focus on habitual criminals.

It would be nice to have a simple theory about what makes criminals begin their life of crime. Instead, criminologists have published a range of theories: peer pressure, genetics, learned behaviors, environment, friends and associates, low self-control, detachment, social discrimination and stereotypes, and response to institutional power. It is complicated.

Crime rates may be down since 1990, but you have not found a simple explanation that points the way for further reductions in crime. For example, look at the scatter-shot list of possible reasons for lower crime rates since 1990 (per Wikipedia):
- Passage of the 1994 Crime Bill
- Increased number of police officers
- Use of data-driven policing practices
- Reduced exposure to lead starting in the 1970s (e.g., paint, gasoline, plumbing materials)
- Higher incarceration rates
- Reduced crack cocaine use
- Security technology (cameras, surveillance)
- Rising income
- Aging population

Why does the US have so many people in prison?
They are not all drug offenders. Roughly a fifth of those in local, state, and federal facilities are there for

drug offences. It is not due to "Three Strikes" policy. The length of sentences is not that much longer now than in previous decades.

High prison populations are mainly due to a higher percentage of convictions resulting in prison sentences.

So, what do prisons do for society?

Purpose of Prisons	Description
Deterrence	discourage people from committing crimes
Punishment	emotional consequences (take away freedom), not physical pain
Rehabilitation	change behaviors to help prisoners return to society without committing more crimes
Incapacitation	isolate criminals apart from society so they cannot commit crimes

What is wrong with prisons?
Prisons and jails are unfair for minorities and people who are poor. Non-Asian minorities are more likely to be sentenced, and receive longer sentences, than whites for the same crimes. Per the Bureau of Justice Statistics, Black imprisonment rate is more than five times that of whites. Poor people who cannot afford bail end up spending more time in jail. As they wait for a hearing, they may lose their jobs. Without income they fall behind on rent and car payments and their families suffer.

VALUES

To say that we need to be tough on crime sounds simple, but tackling crime is complex. The cost, fairness, and effectiveness of incarceration is worrisome. As is the reality that many crimes are never reported - particularly domestic violence.

You decide to list the key steps in the crime-fighting process to see how various criminology policy initiatives match up. You can see how prison is a small part of the crime-fighting process.

Process Step	Example Policy Initiatives
Prevention	Stress management training
	Interpersonal skills training
Detection	Job training
	Monitor repeat offenders
Capture	Cameras in public places
	Facial recognition tracking
	Enforce restraining orders
Prosecution	Security systems at work and home
Punishment	Childcare support for single parents
	Financial support for families of
Rehabilitation	offenders
	E-carceration vs jail or prison
	Public mental health facilities
Re-entry	Funding for addiction treatment
	Support employment for people with criminal records
	Transition housing in safe neighborhoods

You start to see how values tend to drive public policy related to crime. Incarceration responds to our values of security and safety - let's just prosecute and punish the bad guys. To do better at catching bad guys, we could put security cameras on every street, and track everyone like they do in a Las Vegas casino. But that has some privacy issues. Besides, prisons are overcrowded and expensive. Is locking up even more people the answer?

Preventing crimes and rehabilitating offenders requires that we prioritize softer values (empathy, charity, mental and physical wellness, forgiveness). To prevent someone from committing their first crime, they need support, opportunities, and jobs. E-carceration (wearing an ankle tracker) may feel like inadequate punishment. However, to break the cycle of recidivism, society must pursue rehabilitation and re-entry and accept the risk that some ex-convicts will commit heinous crimes.

Key points:
- Data and statistics about crime are incomplete
- There are no simple answers. Our criminal justice system is flawed and over-worked.
- Policy solutions for crime can be expensive and cause unintended consequences
- While this case study started with you pretending to do research over a weekend, consider taking up the cudgel in real life.
- Don't give up. Do more research. Pick a specific issue (e.g., domestic violence). Find people who are making positive changes happen. Help them make a difference.

II. Why People Disagree

Where we use the Opinion-Framework to help diagnose disagreements. Disagreements arise when there is misalignment of supporting-beliefs that two people have about a topic. This insight makes us better prepared to resolve disputes. We can predict when disagreements are likely to be unresolvable. We choose to be OK with that.

Applying the Framework

Refresher on Opinions
Opinions are belief-statements about how things are, how things should be, how things will be, or why things in the past were the way they were. An opinion is supported by a collection of beliefs. To make sense of someone's opinion, it helps to categorize their supporting beliefs into Data, Models, and Values.

Simple as that.

Most Opinions are Under-Cooked
Earlier in this book we listed some examples of the dozens of topics about which we might be expected to have an opinion. You might have snappy answers to questions like where you want to live, who you want to vote for, or do you believe in God. However, developing a complete set of beliefs (that cover data, models, and values) to justify these snappy opinions can be overwhelming.

As a result, most of our opinions are vague and unsupported until we're challenged and must defend our opinion. We might have a few topics that are near and dear to us where we have fully fleshed out opinions with supporting beliefs. Podcasters, talk radio hosts, and consultants formulate and justify opinions for a living. They are pros. We are amateurs. Defending opinions is hard work.

"I tried to explain, but they just don't get it"

We all make the mistake of thinking that facts and data are all we need in order to convince people to agree with us.

A friend of yours wonders why her customers "don't get it" when she patiently explains the benefits of a heat pump for their homes. It is not enough to list the ways that heat pumps can save money and energy. Your friend may need to address the mental model people may have about how heat pumps work, especially in winter. For example, she could encourage her customers to hold their hand over a refrigerator's exhaust vent - feel the heat extracted from a freezer. Your friend would do well to appeal to a customer's core value of what a "home" means to them. Make the point that a heat pump is reliable and makes a home more comfortable or healthier.

New car dealers are masterful at hitting the mark on data, models, and values. They can list the specifications of a car (mileage, 0 to 60 acceleration, cubic feet of cargo space). They can translate that data into a mental model of performance. If you are young and single, acceleration means getting places fast. If you are a parent with small children, acceleration means being able to merge on to a speeding freeway safely. As for core values, car dealers know that a car is an extension of who you are and how you want people to perceive you.

Disagreements - When Opinions Collide

A "difference of opinion" can be represented as two opinion belief-statements that conflict. It can be further represented as misalignment of the supporting belief-statements for each opinion. Sorting belief-statements into data, models, and values categories makes it easier to illustrate that misalignment.

Differences of opinion can be innocuous and dormant. They become "disagreements" when they impact our lives. You could write a book about why people disagree.

We want people to get along. When there is a disagreement, we want to fix it. With enough time and effort, we should be able to get two people to agree, right?

No.

Try a thought experiment. Imagine putting two people who disagree with each other into a locked room with a phone and internet access. Tell them they don't get lunch (soup and a sandwich) until they have an agreement. They have a few hours to reconcile misalignment of their data, models, and values beliefs.

If these two people are open-minded and well-intentioned, then there is a good chance that they can do some research and hash out a common view of facts and data. They might even be able to agree on what models of cause and effect apply to their dispute. However, it is likely that they will deadlock if they differ as to what core values apply and how much more important some values are than others to this disagreement.

No soup for them.

Until you dive into the basis of a disagreement, it is tempting to believe that a simple resolution is possible. The more you know about a topic, the more complex and nuanced it seems. The more entangled people are (families, close-knit work teams), the more complicated their disagreements become.

What is driving a disagreement?

Data-driven. What type of car should we buy? You would think that a married couple should be able to focus on data to make this decision - evaluating features and upgrades versus price. However, before visiting a car dealer, they had better discuss what performance they want from a car (mental model). Also, they need to talk ahead of time to ensure that neither spouse will be embarrassed (self-esteem value) to be seen driving the minivan that facts and data told them to buy.

Models-driven. Who was the best running back in NFL history? There is plenty of objective DATA, such as yards per carry, or per game, or in a career. The VALUES of the sports fans who disagree are likely aligned: objectivity and fairness in the evaluation. The mental MODELS for assessing athletic performance are the source of disagreement.

Individual rushing statistics are affected by how good the team was (more yards per carry and more carries per game), the style of offense (run vs. pass), different eras (some decades had slogging offenses of three yards and a cloud of dust), and injuries. It is easy to fill an hour of a sports-radio talk show with the-best-running-back debate -- discussing adjustments one should make to player statistics to enable fair comparisons across eras, teams, and styles of play.

Values-driven. Should I let my teenager go rock-climbing? How should we resolve a parent's core value of safety versus a teenager's values of adventure and associating with friends? Keeping a child in a bubble, safe from every risk, is a disservice. As a child matures, parents must expand their risk-tolerance: toddlers near hard furniture, riding a bike, walking to school. The rock-climbing discussion will likely focus on risk-mitigation: safety equipment, level of experience of the climbers, maybe a satellite phone.

Key points:
- Developing a robust opinion with solid supporting-beliefs takes some skill and hard work
- Simple disagreements might be data-driven
- Disagreements within a field of expertise tend to be models-driven
- Long-running policy disagreements tend to be values-driven and can be the most difficult to resolve

Diagnosing Disagreements

Let's look at some ways of thinking where we can apply some Opinion-Framework techniques to help understand the nature of disagreements.

Put Flesh on the Bones of the Framework.

Consider a married couple, mid-career, with school-age children. Both spouses work. Spouse A has a career opportunity that requires relocating to a different city, longer working hours, and more business travel. Spouse B wants to discuss this decision. You have been asked to help them make the decision. To get the conversation rolling, you plan to ask them to list some factors that are relevant to the decision. As you prep for the meeting, you jot down some data, models, and values ideas they are likely to bring up:

<u>Element</u>	<u>Factors to Consider</u>
Data	Cost of living in current and new locations
	Moving and transition costs
	Quality of school systems
	Status of children's friendships and school work
	Spouse A career - incremental benefit of new job vs current job
	Spouse B career - potential if stay

Element	Factors to Consider
Models	Difficulty for Spouse B to find employment
	Reduction in time Spouse A will have for parenting
	Impact of a move on children - social, psychological, educational
	Expectations - how often should they relocate during their working lives
	Parity - What if Spouse B gets an offer in a few years that can't be refused?
Values	Financial security
	Marriage equity
	Life-Work balance
	Raising children well
	Emotional Roots - any connections to current or new location?

Degree of Alignment

When two people disagree, don't expect them to disagree about every bit of data or logic. There can be significant overlaps in the beliefs they have. Imagine you have interviewed two people, one in favor of, and one opposed to, the death penalty. Here is a concise way to capture the degree of misalignment of belief statements – and identify focus areas for resolving a disagreement. Notice how much two people who have a strong difference of opinion can be aligned on their supporting-beliefs.

Element	For	Against	Beliefs about the Death Penalty
Data	Yes	Yes	Death row incarceration costs more than life without parole
	No	Yes	Has no effect on murder rates
	Maybe	Yes	Too many innocent people are on death row
	Yes	No	Humane methods of execution are available
Models	Yes	No	Deters capital crimes
	Maybe	Yes	Unfair due to race, geography, quality of lawyers
	No	Yes	Form of cruel punishment
	Yes	Maybe	Brings closure to victim's families
	Maybe	Yes	Arbitrary in practice - inconsistent penalties for same crimes
	Yes	Yes	Juveniles and mentally ill should not be executed
Values	No	Yes	All life is worth saving
	Yes	No	Justice and retribution (eye for an eye)
	Maybe	Yes	Mercy and redemption (forgiveness)

Element	For	Against	Beliefs about the Death Penalty
	Maybe	Yes	Arbitrary and discriminatory penalties violate human rights

In the case of the death penalty, proponents may support capital punishment even if they concede that: death row is more expensive than life without parole, the death penalty does not deter capital crimes, and sentencing is arbitrary and unfair.

Complexity and Evolution of a Debate

A disagreement or debate may evolve as society and technology change. We don't view abortion in the same way as our ancestors did.

Abortion methods have been used for thousands of years and have had varying levels of effectiveness and safety:

- Herbal plants or chemicals (e.g., pennyroyal, turpentine)
- Pressure or trauma to the abdomen (e.g., tight corset, striking the stomach or falling)
- Surgery (e.g., inserting a catheter, injecting hot water, dilation and curettage)

The abortion debate might have been straightforward in 1820. People for and against abortion were debating opposite sides of the same coin.

Some widely-held belief-statements related to abortion at that time might have included:

Element	Belief Statements circa 1820
Data	Birth control methods are not very effective
	Both abortions and births are high risk for women
	Women's rights are limited (e.g., owning property, voting)
	Life begins at quickening
Models	Husbands must give permission for an abortion
	Abortions prior to quickening are not homicides
	Midwives and medical practitioners are qualified to perform abortions
Values	Sanctity of life
	Role of women in the family
	Religious obedience

Until the mid-1800s, abortion was legal and roughly one-fifth of pregnancies were terminated. Abortion death rates were high. But when done by a skilled practitioner, abortion risks were comparable to giving birth.

Gradually, abortion was criminalized through the late 1800s. The medical profession wanted to put abortion practitioners out of business. Opponents of women's rights wanted to restrict women's autonomy.

In the early 1900s, the pendulum swung back, somewhat, toward legalizing abortions. By then, the risks of abortions and births were lower for women who had money and access to reputable doctors.

Tragically, for most women, unsafe illegal abortions were common.

After Roe v. Wade, the abortion rights debate evolved and became more complex. Three drivers of that complexity come to mind: medical science, technology, and women's rights. Medical science has made people question when life begins (not just "quickening"). Technology has redesigned sexual reproduction (safer and more effective birth control, fertility treatments, and abortion pills). Women's-rights policies enabled women to have more control of their bodies. Reframed as Pro-Life versus Pro-Choice, supporters and opponents of abortion rights are no longer describing opposite sides of the same coin.

Unintended Consequences

When you win a debate, there can be unintended consequences for your success. Careful what you wish for.

Alcohol consumption has been a public health issue in the US since the first European settlers arrived. In the 18th and 19th centuries, Americans drank a lot of alcohol, which was usually safer than plain water. While consuming alcohol was accepted and encouraged, public drunkenness was not.

Temperance movements ebbed and flowed in US history. Everyone realized how tragic alcoholism could be. In years prior to Prohibition, many dry counties and states had local versions of prohibition. The high-water mark of Temperance was Prohibition at a national level, from 1920 to 1933.

A few belief statements that supported Temperance and the 18th Amendment:

Element	Belief Statements for Prohibition
Data	Working class alcohol use correlated with crime and disorderliness Circa 1918, job growth was driven by urban factories Income Tax revenues (legalized in 1913) could replace lost excise taxes from alcohol
Models	Saloons are a tool of brewers and a source of political mischief Drunkenness causes unemployment, domestic violence, and an unhealthy saloon-culture Physical health improves with moderate drinking or abstinence from alcohol. Factory jobs are more unsafe than other jobs when workers are intoxicated With Prohibition, people will be healthier, crime will go down, workers will be safer and more productive, and families will avoid financial ruin.
Values	Social order and decorum Family Public safety Religious faith and piety

Prohibition led to some unintended consequences. Enforcement resources (e.g., revenue agents) were inadequate. Public support for enforcing the law waned. Prohibition normalized ordinary Americans' breaking the law. Loopholes in the law favored the rich and caused unrest among working poor. Alcohol consumption did drop in the short run, but Americans who wanted alcohol could get what they wanted through legal and illegal sources. The better world promised by the Temperance movement did not materialize.

Anti-prohibition activism gained momentum when the Depression started. Tax revenues declined during the Depression (a lot of income-tax-paying jobs were lost). The government needed the excise taxes that legal alcohol could generate. Ratified on December 5, 1933, the 21st amendment repealed the 18th amendment.

The national experiment of Prohibition as a constitutional solution was a failure. However, Temperance is alive and well at the state and local levels. More than a third of the US population currently live in localities that are dry or "damp."

Key points:
- As you would expect, this book's Opinion-Framework helps unpack disagreements (wouldn't that be embarrassing were it otherwise!)
- People who disagree may be more aligned in their supporting-beliefs than you might expect
- You should expect long-lived disagreements to evolve and cause unintended consequences

Resolving Disagreements - Formal Methods

Without a process and an authority empowered to render a decision, disagreements can be endless. Most informal disagreements are resolved through power. Within a family, parents try to have the final say. In a business, senior executives give orders and hope that they are followed.

There are circumstances where a disagreement should be resolved in a fair manner where the interests of all parties are considered. Formal methods for resolving disagreements are effective when parties consent to abide by the outcome. By the way, "resolving" a disagreement does not mean that the parties involved "agree" with each other!

Often, you will not have the benefit of formal authority. Nevertheless, let's see what we can learn from a few of these formal methods.

Public Hearings

Local government committees, school boards, and homeowner associations are examples of organizations that have formal hearings and public comment periods to provide a voice for constituents. There is no promise that these organizations will act upon what they hear.

There is a balance between free speech and conducting business. So, these organizations can restrict the topics discussed and the time allowed for a person to provide comments. They are not allowed to exclude people with opposing viewpoints.

For people who speak at a public hearing, there are ways to be more effective. Extreme emotion and disruptiveness may alienate even the decision-makers who are already on your side. Be concise, polite, calm, organized and logical. Tell a story, be relevant to the topic, and establish credibility. Most importantly, explain exactly how what you are saying should influence the outcome of the decision at hand.

Debate Techniques

Competitive debates have a tight structure.

Two teams compete. There is a judge who keeps score and decides on the winner. The debate topic is provided. There may be limited time to prepare. The proposition team argues in favor, and the opposition team against. Each team has time slots to make their case with "constructive" speeches, introducing evidence (data) and logic (mental models). Then, each team makes a "rebuttal" speech that summarizes their views and pokes at the other team's points.

These are not flowery Lincoln-Douglas debate speeches. Competitive debate-speak does not work well in ordinary discussions. Debaters rapid-fire as many supportive points and zingers as they can in the time allotted. However, debating develops valuable skills such as research, public speaking, formulating questions, handling hecklers and interjections, and composure under pressure.

Courtrooms

In a court of law there are a lot of rules and norms. There is a judge to manage the process, and decisions are rendered by the judge or a jury. Attorneys usually represent the clients - plaintiff and defense. Plaintiffs have the burden of proof, making their case beyond reasonable doubt or based on the preponderance of evidence. Defense responds. Plaintiffs have the last word - rebuttal.

During a trial, several elements need to be communicated: the accusation, applicable law, evidence (DATA), logic and reasoning (MODELS) linking the accused to the offense, and damages and harm resulting from the offense. The bulk of a trial is the presentation of evidence and testimony of witnesses. Attorneys use opening and closing arguments to tell the story.

It is rare for a member of the jury to be undecided during closing arguments. So, the purpose of a closing argument is not to win over members of the jury who are against you. Instead, you are providing, to members of the jury who agree with you, a story they can repeat during deliberations. Closing arguments require skills like being organized, keeping things simple and memorable, being specific. Attorneys use a logical flow that integrates the evidence and theories presented and connects with the jury's own experience. When you are in a debate-like situation and acting like a lawyer, be confident about your case, but admit any weaknesses, and build empathy for your client.

Arbitration

The next time you are online and clicking on the box that says you have read the terms and conditions document, read it. There is likely a clause about arbitration as a means to resolve disputes. Arbitration can be binding (no recourse and the decision is final) or non-binding (you have the option to file a lawsuit if you don't like the decision).

Arbitration avoids the cost and time associated with lawsuits. A neutral arbitrator listens to both sides in a dispute and renders a decision. Arbitrators have a lot of power. They set deadlines and rules for the process. They listen to (or read) what the parties present to support their case. Arbitrators then write a document with their final opinions and directed outcomes. The experience is faster and less expensive than a court case.

Media Training

To win in the court of public opinion, participants in a disagreement must develop communication skills. Media personalities and editors have a lot of power to define an issue. You probably don't have much experience participating in media communications. However, you might be unlucky enough to find yourself on the wrong end of an interview for a videocast or a written article. Don't freeze up.

Here are some lessons-learned for doing well in such an interview:

Preparing	Have goals for the interview or press release

	Know your audience
	Prepare and practice in advance of media interactions. Anticipate difficult questions
	Learn to control body language
Answering	Understand the question
	Be concise
	Answer the question, or roll on to answer the question you wanted to answer
	If you don't know the answer to a question, admit it, then roll on to make the point you want to make
	Avoid answering hypothetical questions
Managing the Message	Don't make promises you can't keep
	Be calm, assertive, friendly, positive
	Repeat key message points and keep them sounding fresh
	Be responsive and empathetic with media representatives, understand their world

Key points:
- Formal methods for resolving disagreements have processes and rules that help force a *resolution*, which may not mean that the parties involved *agree* with the outcome
- The skills needed to develop a case and win over decision-makers in formal situations are also useful for informal dispute resolution

Winning Arguments vs Changing Minds

Our Winning Culture

Every event seems to have winners and losers, and somebody wants you to know about it. Pay attention to clickbait news headlines that start with the words "Winners and losers in yesterday's ..." These headlines cover every topic: Congressional budget talks, the NFL draft, stock market movements, Paris fashion week, Supreme Court decisions. Content creators seem compelled to provide instant analysis. Even sporting events have in-game win-probability charts - it's not enough to just watch the game.

When someone "wins" an argument, someone else "loses." Winning is normally a matter of power. (Power as a means of influence and manipulation is covered in a later chapter.) In a disagreement, those with power win.

In the short run, people without power must accept the outcomes of losing. In the long run, those without power have two options. They can gradually change the attitudes and beliefs of their opponents. Or, they can find and leverage other sources of power, such as lawsuits, regulators, key customers, and labor unions.

Compromise may not be an Option

When power is more balanced between two parties in a disagreement, then negotiations and compromise can result in an agreement. Negotiating takes time. Compromise requires give and take. In our society, the shift in our culture toward a "winners and losers" mindset has made compromise and negotiation more difficult.

In politics, there used to be partisan power but a willingness to get things done. The 1986 Tax Reform Act took a few years of committee hearings and bipartisan negotiations. It may not be possible in the current political landscape to spend months, much less years, developing major legislation. A politician who has an open-minded conversation with a member of the opposite party might be branded a traitor. Daily social media posts by politicians and policy thought leaders limit thoughtful debate. Brinksmanship is in fashion: no compromise, no negotiation.

Changing Minds - The Hardest Path

Changing people's opinions is hard work and can be slow-going. It is often not worth the effort. Change must come from within - that is, starting with people's values. Then, their mental models need to be challenged. Finally, facts and data must be reassessed.

To show how hard inducing change can be, let's explore a lengthy example. Imagine a relative of yours is an active investor. He loves the control and freedom of managing his money. He believes that his research gives him an edge over other investors - who he calls sheep or "dumb money." He participates in online investor communities. Buying and selling stocks is exciting.

You are worried. He tells stories about a perfect trade or how he beat the market. Yet, he is a little vague when comparing his long-term results to benchmarks. Recently, he is sounding like a gambler chasing losses.

Do you really want to change his mind about investing? He may get angry at your "intervention." Still, he is married to your cousin. His actions affect her. You feel you must act.

It is tempting to start with data about investment management. You might explain that most professional fund managers do not beat the market. Stock volatility is greater and more skewed than most people understand. You could show him how passive index investing should give him a better long-term return, less stress, and more time for his family.

Lecturing him about the risks of his investor-mindset won't work. Instead, get him to talk about his mental models, then elicit which of his core values are in play. "Models" means the tools, methods, insights, and skills he claims give him an edge. "Values" means what drives his behavior, such as control, thrill of winning, reputation with peers, or distrust of experts.

If your cousin's spouse truly believes he is good at investing, he should rise to the challenge of proving himself. First, force him to write down his philosophy in black and white. Second, demand that he work with a neutral third party who would monitor his performance. Until he proves his methods are effective, he should be willing to agree to actively manage only a small portion of his assets while putting the rest of his money into index funds.

Your cousin's financial well-being is worth the effort. Success depends on your being able to leverage the investor's pride to force him to prove that his methods work. In the meantime, he should be happy enough to play in a small sandbox of a brokerage account and not put all of his net worth at risk.

Changing behavior can require tough love and an intervention. You would need to build trust or find a relationship coach who can help your cousin reset the terms of her marriage. Good luck with that!

Key points:
- Power is the easiest way to get what you want
- Negotiation and compromise are possible when two parties have something to trade
- Changing someone's opinions and behaviors is very difficult

Living with Unresolved Disagreements

Most disagreements that are tied to core values or deeply rooted mental models are never resolved. Don't be sad. Letting go of "we should all get along" is empowering and healthy.

Try Doing Nothing - Leave it Be
The idealized vision of a happy marriage has no conflict. On the contrary, every long-term personal relationship has disagreements. Some of those disagreements are serious and never resolved.

Examples of unresolved disagreements include, do we have enough money, should we move to a bigger home, you drink too much, you aren't home enough, I really need a sports car, you never want sex, you listen to your parents more than to me, you belittle my contributions to this relationship.

These types of disagreements will probably not be resolved. Instead, the people involved will work out tradeoffs and compromises and carry on.

Is "Agree to Disagree" even a thing?
When emotions get intense during an argument, someone will say, "Then let's just agree to disagree." The full meaning of that phrase is that we will stop arguing and tolerate each other's point of view. It is

the tolerance piece that is often overlooked. Most "agree to disagree" outcomes are a pause in the battle.

If two people on opposite sides of an issue can proceed with everyday life, and their disagreements don't interfere with what they want to do, then they are qualified to agree to disagree. On the other hand, people who refuse to compromise, and people who hate, are not capable of tolerance. When they pause a battle and agree to disagree, they are, in fact, reloading.

Accommodation

Accommodating unresolved disagreements means adjusting one's actions and goals. The burden of accommodation usually rests with those who have less power. In some cases, accommodating an insensitive person takes a lot of effort and can dominate day-to-day life.

Problem Behavior	Accommodations
Spendthrift spouses	Automatically pay bills and set aside money Limits on credit cards
Disorganized bosses	Screen their email and calendar Appoint a chief of staff or aide-de-camp Figure out who to blame when things go wrong
Loud neighbors	Avoid setting them off Tall shrubs and fences Headphones Stay indoors Move to a new neighborhood

Problem Behavior	Accommodations
Career that requires frequent relocation	Get good at packing and moving Minimize furniture and belongings Home-school the kids Be able to make friends quickly (e.g., through sports and hobbies)

Ultimatums

Some disagreements are unacceptable and cannot be accommodated. In a negotiation, you must be willing to walk away. Likewise, when faced with a make-or-break unresolvable disagreement, leaving home or a marriage or a job may be the best outcome.

Key points:
- Living with unresolved disagreements is ubiquitous
- There is no shame or failure in not resolving a disagreement as long as there is mutual respect
- When people reach their limits, it is time to go

Case Study: Disdain

Can you disagree with someone who does not feel you are worthy?

Some people are polite. They will listen to what you have to say. Other people will listen to you if you have power or a strong argument. Then, there are people who do not care what you think.

There is research demonstrating that disdain is a reliable signal that a relationship is heading for trouble. We can use three connotations of disdain, that range from mild to offensive, to explore how disdain presents itself and what we can do about it.

Dismissiveness includes taking people for granted and not valuing their input or presence. Being dismissive does not require much emotional energy.

Contempt is a stronger form of disdain. It requires some energy and emotion to muster the scorn that contempt implies.

Dehumanization goes beyond disdain. It taps into hatred and stereotypes. Dehumanization requires a lot of emotional energy.

How to recognize practitioners of disdain:

Data	Use false data and stereotypes Identify a reason why someone is beneath them

Models	Treat people who provide a service as objects Spread rumors and conspiracy theories Portray people who are different as a threat
Values	Superiority Power Tribalism Status quo

Dismissiveness

If you don't have frequent interactions with someone, you can be dismissive. Why be nice and courteous to restaurant workers, field laborers, taxi drivers, supermarket checkout employees, or customer service reps? Notice how name tags, and introducing themselves, can change the dynamic for these people with their customers.

To overcome dismissiveness, be assertive and train others to treat you with respect. Encourage empathy by sharing stories about people's culture and personal lives. Accumulate power (and respect) by building relationships and trading favors that get results. If you can deliver customers, revenues, or votes, then you won't be dismissed anymore.

Contempt

Professor John Gottman led research into marriage and divorce. A key conclusion was that contempt is a leading indicator of divorce. Marriage (as with any intense relationship) takes effort and time. All relationships have conflict, and all relationships have some forms of unresolvable conflict.

Disdain (contempt) is one of the four warning signs in a relationship:

Criticism	verbal attacks that get at a person's core
Contempt	ridicule, insults and verbal abuse
Defensiveness	play the victim and deflect blame
Stonewalling	withdrawal and distraction, shutting down, unresponsiveness

Source: gottman.com

Gottman identifies behaviors that can counteract these warning signs:
- Provide feedback on how you feel, not accusations.
- Listen to each other, and take a break when emotions interfere with listening.
- Be supportive. Solve the problems that can be solved, and work to accommodate the problems that cannot be solved.
- Collaborate to make decisions.

Dehumanization

When you call people "vermin" and blame them for whatever is wrong in your life, you are dehumanizing them. Dehumanization enables racism, misogyny, persecution, and genocide. It takes root when people feel threatened. It justifies doing wrong.

In a civilized society, once a category of people is dehumanized, it becomes acceptable to take away their rights, abuse and mistreat them, and even declare all-out war meant to exterminate them

Propaganda is a type of dehumanization tool. It weaponizes words to attack an opponent's sense of self. Decency and civil rights are not necessary when your opponents are sub-human.

What can be done? Teach empathy. Model the Golden Rule. Focus on the behavior that is unacceptable and not the person. Avoid labelling people as if they are animals (vermin), or their illness (addict), or their circumstance (poor).

Key points:
- Disdain is rooted in power
- If you believe that people are beneath you, then you need not bother acknowledging their opinions
- Countering disdain requires assertiveness in personal relationships and empathy in social policy

Case Study: The Federal Budget

Our federal budget is the residue of long-running disagreements between liberals and conservatives. The mental models and values that drive their policies differ as to what role the government should play in our lives (especially regarding regulating business and social welfare programs).

So, let's tackle this intractable public policy debate, in a way that allows us to start forming our own opinions.

Do We Have a Problem?

Deficits have been the norm for many decades. The last surplus was in 2001. In the table below, deficits are shown as a percentage of tax receipts. For example, in 1982, 21% more tax income would have to have been collected to balance the budget. Outlays (government spending) and the federal debt are shown as percentages of GDP. The federal debt is the accumulated net of deficits and surpluses over time.

Federal Tax History: Benchmark to GDP

Year	Deficit as a % of Receipts	Outlays/ GDP	Debt/ GDP
1952	-2%	19%	71%
1957	4%	17%	57%

Year	Deficit as a % of Receipts	Outlays/ GDP	Debt/ GDP
1962	-7%	18%	49%
1967	-6%	19%	38%
1972	-11%	19%	33%
1977	-15%	20%	34%
1982	-21%	23%	34%
1987	-18%	21%	48%
1992	-27%	22%	62%
1997	-1%	19%	63%
2002	-9%	19%	57%
2007	-6%	19%	62%
2012	-44%	22%	99%
2017	-20%	21%	103%
2022	-28%	25%	120%

Source: Bureau of Economic Analysis, treasury.gov

You can see how deficits ebb and flow with recessions, tax cuts, tax credits and government subsidies. Government spending (Outlays) bounce around 20% of GDP plus or minus a few percentage points. Federal debt as a percentage of GDP has had people sounding the alarm for decades. You can see that in 1952, we were still paying off debt from World War Two. Through the early 1980s, our economy grew enough to mask higher deficits. Now, there is nowhere to hide.

Break Down the Federal Budget

In the instructions for your tax return (IRS Form 1040), you will find a summary of the Federal Budget. There are pie charts that break down the Receipts and Outlays. Next tax season, take a minute to look over those charts. The table below shows similar data categories.

Federal Budget Snapshot

($ billions)	1982	2002	2022
GDP	$3,344	$10,929	$25,744
Outlays as % of GDP	22.5%	18.6%	24.8%
Deficit as % of GDP	3.8%	1.4%	5.3%
Receipts	$618	$1,853	$4,897
Individual Income Taxes	48%	46%	54%
Corporation Income Taxes	8%	8%	9%
Social Insurance / Retirement	33%	38%	30%
Excise Taxes	6%	4%	2%
Other	5%	4%	5%
Outlays	$746	$2,011	$6,273
National defense	25%	17%	12%
Human resources	52%	66%	75%
Physical resources	8%	5%	3%
Net interest	11%	9%	8%

($ billions)	1982	2002	2022
Other functions	7%	6%	6%
Undistributed offsets	-4%	-2%	-4%
Deficit	$128	$158	$1,376

Source: Bureau of Economic Analysis, Office of Management and Budget

Observations - Receipts

Individual income taxes are contributing more and more to Receipts than payroll taxes (Social Security and Medicare). Perhaps the rich *are* getting richer.

Why are corporation income taxes not a big source for Receipts? Those taxes are a percentage of *profits*, not revenues. By comparison, if your household were a business, the individual income and payroll taxes you pay would be equivalent to being taxed on your *revenues*.

Let's do a sanity check. Corporation income tax receipts for 2022 were about $440 billion (9% of $4,897 billion). If GDP were one company with $25,744 billion in revenues, and had 10% profit and was taxed at 21%, then GDP's tax would be $540 billion. Only a hundred billion off. The point is, don't expect corporate income taxes to make much of a dent in the deficit. If you want to talk about a value added tax (VAT) to make businesses pay more tax, give it a try. But VAT is more a sales tax paid by consumers than a business tax paid by corporate titans.

Observations - Outlays

Growth in National Defense has been less than inflation. Same for Physical Resources spending (housing, infrastructure). We should keep an eye on Net Interest. It tends to surge with higher interest rates.

The big hitter is Human Resources at 75% of Outlays. It includes Social Security benefits and health programs (such as Medicare, Medicaid, and the Children's Health Insurance Program). It also includes Income Security (assistance for housing and nutrition, unemployment compensation, earned income and child tax credits). Most of the increase in Human Resources as a percentage of GDP has been caused by health care, with an added bump due to pandemic-related unemployment compensation in 2022.

It may help our thinking to categorize Outlays (government spending) into three types:

Category	Description
Wealth Transfer	Social welfare and equity programs. Direct transfer of tax money to beneficiaries.
Gov't Operations	Defense, infrastructure and other activities that are national in scope
Admin and Regulatory	Administrative departments and rulemaking agencies that run the executive branch and implement legislation

If you want to reduce spending, then you must focus on the first two categories of Outlays.

On the contrary, major players in industry who are savvy about policy pay attention to the small budget items in the Admin and Regulatory category.

Buried in Other Functions, there are some small departments and agencies that have tremendous impact through regulation and oversight. For example, we have the departments of Commerce, Energy, Labor, the Environmental Protection Agency, and the Consumer Product Safety Commission. Spending on all these organizations is less than $100 billion (about 1.5% of Outlays). A lot of power, lobbying, and smart-money is directed at Other Functions.

Fair Share of Tax Burden

Let's put some context behind a tax-related headline. You have heard that a small percentage of taxpayers pay a high percentage of income tax generated. True. Less than one percent of taxpayers pay more than a third of total income tax receipts. About 10 percent pay two-thirds.

Let's see for ourselves in the table below. In 2021, there were about 160 million tax returns. The first column lists the tax brackets. The second column shows the percentage of returns filed for each top rate. The third and fourth columns show the percentage of total tax revenues generated by those returns, and their average tax rate.

Income Tax Breakdown by Tax Rate Class

2021	# Returns	Tax Generated	Avg. Income tax rate
Total - all returns	160 million	$2.28 trillion	19.4%
Tax Rate Class:			
0 percent	20.1%	0.0%	0.0%
10 percent	15.5%	0.7%	9.3%
12 percent	33.1%	8.7%	11.0%
22 percent	19.5%	18.8%	14.7%
24 percent	6.7%	16.7%	18.5%
32 percent	1.0%	4.8%	21.1%
35 percent	1.1%	9.3%	24.5%
37 percent	0.7%	35.9%	30.2%
Capital Gains + Child returns	2.2%	5.1%	16.1%

Source: IRS

By way of example, people in the 32 percent marginal tax rate bracket filed 1% of all returns, paid 4.8% of all taxes, and paid an average tax rate of 21.1%.

Before we pity high earners, let's include payroll tax and look at a more complete picture of tax burden by tax bracket. We'll look at six hypothetical taxpayers, whose taxable incomes (for ordinary rates) are at the top of the single-payer tax brackets for 2022. Then, we'll include the effect of the standard deduction ($12,950) to get an estimate for gross earned income that is used for payroll taxes.

Three kinds of income for taxpayers:

Marginal Rate	Taxable Income (Form 1040)	Payroll income (Medicare)	Social Security Income
10%	$10,275	$23,225	$23,225
12%	$41,775	$54,725	$54,725
22%	$89,075	$102,025	$102,025
24%	$170,050	$183,000	$147,000
32%	$215,950	$228,900	$147,000
35%	$539,900	$552,850	$147,000

Your payroll taxes are paid half by you and half by your employer (self-employed pay it all). Medicare tax is 1.45% for each of you and your employer, on all your earned income (plus and extra 0.9% withheld on income over $200,000). Social security is 6.2% each for you and your employer, up to the $147,000 income limit.

By way of example, we are saying that a taxpayer whose taxable income on their 1040 is $215,950 Is at the top of the 32% tax bracket. Add back the standard deduction of $12,950 for single-a person household to estimate the Medicare payroll taxable income. This person's income Exceeds the Social Security income level so only $147,000 is subject to that tax.

To spare you some math, here are the results. There are three columns showing taxes paid as a percentage of "gross Income" (the payroll tax column, above). The first data column is just income tax paid by each taxpayer. The second column is income tax plus payroll tax paid by the taxpayers - what they feel in their Wallets. Finally, the third column includes the employer portion of payroll tax, to reflect what the government receives in total on behalf of each taxpayer.

Marginal Rate	Income tax	Wallet	Government
10%	4.4%	12.1%	19.7%
12%	8.8%	16.4%	24.1%
22%	14.9%	22.6%	30.2%
24%	18.9%	25.4%	31.8%
32%	21.6%	27.0%	32.5%
35%	29.4%	32.5%	36.2%

The government makes good money from lower income taxpayers. By having payroll tax payments split between individuals and their employers, the government has cleverly softened the blow of how taxes are perceived by taxpayers.

Key points:
- If the federal government were a household, it would have trouble qualifying for a loan
- Social Services has grown as a % of GDP and Congress has refused to generate enough tax revenue to cover those commitments

- People talk about government waste and spending, but the smart-money focuses on the small regulatory departments and agencies
- To get a clearer picture of who is paying their fair share of taxes, pay attention to both income and payroll taxes.
- Don't expect corporate taxes to significantly reduce deficits.

Case Study: Social Security

This chapter may feel excruciating, but it is intended to help you think for yourself about a political hot potato that is personal for you. Pay attention to rhetoric, blame, and inertia as we approach depletion of the trust fund. If you have ever paid payroll taxes, go to the social security website and look at your statement. (Please do it now before you read another word.)

Original Intent
During the Depression in the 1930s about half of elderly people lived in poverty. The Social Security Act of 1935 was designed to be a "self-supporting" safety net. Social Security avoided being called "welfare," because it was not paid out of general revenues. Payroll taxes from working people would pay for benefits given to retired people over 65 years old. Only about half the jobs in the US were included originally by social security. Farm and domestic workers, for example, were not included.

Expansion
Over time, Social Security was expanded to include spouses and families of workers, then disability was

added. So, the full name for social security is "Old-Age, Survivors, and Disability Insurance."

Changes to the benefit levels were haphazard until 1972, when automatic cost-of-living adjustments were implemented. Prior to then, Congress had to pass legislation for each one-off increase.

Changes to the payroll tax rate are still defined by statute (6.2% each for employee and employer, so 12.4% combined). Note in the table below that for a generation, payroll tax rate increases were common. However, the current tax rate has held steady since 1990.

OASDI combined (employer + employee) tax rate history

Years	OASDI combined tax rate
1937 to 1949	2%
1950 to 1953	3%
1954 to 1989	From 4% to 12.12% (18 rate changes)
1990 to present	12.4%

Source: SSA and taxpolicycenter.org

Life Expectancy

In 1935, life expectancy at birth was about 62 years, compared to roughly 78 years today. For the first few decades of the 20th century, life expectancy was affected by infant and child mortality. What matters for social security is life expectancy once a person reaches adulthood. Men aged 65 in 1935 could expect to live another 13 years versus 18 years today.

In 1983, Congress passed a law to increase the full retirement age (FRA) for social security, taking effect 20 years after the law passed. The FRA gradually increased from 65 to 67 in two five-year waves - starting with people turning 65 in 2003 and finishing with people turning 65 in 2025. It might be difficult to sell an immediate increase in FRAs.

Trust Funds

You will see headlines declaring that Social Security is going bankrupt. Not true. What is true is that the trust funds have started to decline. If the trust funds run out of money, then social security benefits would be reduced (perhaps roughly 20%).

There are two OASDI Trust Funds. The Old-Age and Survivors Insurance (OASI) Trust and the Disability Insurance (DI) Trust. The OASI Trust is much bigger (20+ times larger) than the DI Trust. These trusts receive excess payroll tax and invest in government-backed Treasuries.

In the early 1980's, social security faced an acute funding crisis. Congress acted to shore up social security in 1983, based on input from a Commission chaired by Alan Greenspan. In addition to increasing the full retirement age, the Greenspan commission recommended taxing social security benefits for higher income individuals and increased the payroll tax.

For more than a decade, we have experienced déjà vu in slow motion. Like the early 1980's, in 2009, benefits began to exceed payroll tax income. However, interest income covered the difference for a dozen years. In 2021, total costs exceeded total income and reserves covered the shortfall. Relative to total cost, reserves were much higher in 2022 than in 1982. Nonetheless, without any action by Congress to address social security, the reserves might only last until the early 2030s - at which point Social Security would not go "bankrupt." Benefits would be reduced to 75% to 80% of current levels.

Worker to Beneficiary Ratio

After it began in 1937, social security took a few decades to achieve a "steady-state" balance of workers to beneficiaries. By 1970, newly retired people had spent most of their careers paying into social security. The ratio of workers to beneficiaries (W/B) was a comfortable 3.7. A sustainable W/B ratio might be roughly 3.0, plus or minus.

The steady downward trend for the W/B ratio is primarily due to birth-rate declines. "Crude birth-rate" (births per 1000 population) has dropped more than half since 1950. Declining immigration and increasing life expectancy are lesser drivers of W/B. The W/B ratio is expected to drop further to 2.3 by 2040, which makes sense since the birthrates of 2010 and 2020 will impact the worker population by 2030 to 2040.

Worker to Beneficiary ratio history

Year	W/B Ratio	Crude Birth-Rate
1950	16.5	24.1
1960	5.1	23.7
1970	3.7	18.4

Year	W/B Ratio	Crude Birth-Rate
1980	3.2	15.9
1990	3.4	16.7
2000	3.4	14.4
2010	2.9	11.2
2020	2.7	11.0

Source: SSA 2022 Trustees Report, CDC

How Social Security benefits are calculated

The Social Security Administration (SSA) tracks your taxable income and payroll taxes and can provide an estimate of your expected benefit. You really should have your Social Security statement in hand before you keep reading. Key vocabulary:

Base Earnings. Each year you work has a Maximum Taxable Earnings limit. That number is both the contribution base and the benefit base. For example, in 2022, the contribution base was $147,000, and any income over that amount was free from the 6.2% payroll deduction. That same $147,000 limit is the baseline for calculating monthly benefits for retirees who turned 60 years old in 2022.

AIME. Average Indexed Monthly Earnings (AIME). Average of your top 35 years' income (adjusted for inflation) as calculated during the year you turn 60.

PIA. Primary Insurance Amount (PIA). Your monthly benefit that you get if you start drawing social security at your full retirement age (67 for people born after 1960).

Bend Points. Your PIA is a percentage of the base earnings. Rather than have a single flat percent of earnings, there are three PIA factors. The bend points divide up the base earnings into three ranges.

As an example, assume a retiree using 2022 assumptions has a lifetime monthly AIME earnings of $7,000. The monthly benefit base is $12,252 ($147,000/12). This retiree could have made more than $147,000 in later years and been above the max earnings for payroll tax for some years. But, early in his or her career, there were probably a lot of years with a lot less than the max earnings.

Here is the math for building up to the PIA benefit.

Bend Point Ranges	PIA Factor	AIME	PIA
Up to $1,024	90%	$1,024	$922
$1,024 to $6,172	32%	$5,148	$1,647
$6,172 to $12,250	15%	$828	$124
	Total	$7,000	$2,693

So, adjusting for inflation, this retiree averaged $84,000 per year ($7,000 x 12). He or she has a target Social Security benefit of $32,316 per year ($2,693 x 12). Not enough to live on, but good money that will increase with annual inflation adjustments.

Comparing Your Contributions to Your Benefits

The PIA factors are designed to give beneficiaries who make less career earnings a higher percentage of their earnings back as a benefit. In this case, the retiree is getting 38.5% of earnings back ($2,693/ $7,000). If this retiree's earnings had maxed out the contribution base (giving an AIME of $12,250), then the PIA would be $3,481 (28.4% of earnings). The higher your earnings, the lower your benefit is as a percentage of earnings. Don't despair if your earnings are low. The benefit is still generous.

Compare the benefit percentage in the example (38.5%) to the payroll tax rate (12.4% combined for employee and employer). The retiree is getting three times as much back each year as was paid in.

Not bad.

Think of the benefit percentage compared to what you pay in (12.4%) this way. If you could keep what you and your employer pay in to social security, you could work for about 40 years until retirement and save 12.4% of your income each year. Assume your investments keep up with inflation. Then, when you retire with a life expectancy of 20 years, you could withdraw the equivalent of 24.8% (twice what you paid in) of your average annual income before you run out of cash. Social Security benefit percentages are better than 24.8% at all earnings levels, which is good for a low-risk return on investment.

Inescapable Math

Since the early 1980's the bend points and PIA benefit factors have been consistent. Year after year, the PIA factors have been 90%, 32%, and 15%, and the bend points have been the nearly the same percentages of the benefit base 8.4% ($1,024/ $12,250) and 50.4% ($6,172/ $12,250). The benefit base ($147,000 for 2022) goes up each year per an inflation index.

Not only is the worker/ beneficiary ratio an issue. There is a little kicker when it comes to earnings. From 1982 to 2022, the benefit base (Social Security Maximum Earnings limit) has increased by a factor of about 4.5 times, while household earnings and wages per job have not kept up (about 3.7 times). That means less payroll taxes collected per household now and higher PIA benefit percentages for retirees in the future.

Back to the MODEL: Safety Net or Retirement Plan

We saw in a previous chapter that social security seems to have had an impact on elderly poverty rates. In the early 1960s, poverty for people over age 65 was above 30%, and has been at or below 10% since the year 2000.

In 2021, per census.gov poverty tables, about 8.5 million people over the age of 65 lived below 125% of the poverty threshold. 80% of their income came from social security. Let's look at our 2022 example to compare a poverty level to social security benefits.

The 2022 Federal Poverty Level (FPL) was $13,590 ($1,132 per month) for a single person household. In the retiree example above, the first bend point PIA of $922 per month is about 80% of FPL, and the second bend point benefit of $2,569 ($922 + $1,647) is more than twice the FPL.

Social security is designed to help people earn enough benefits to stay out of poverty in retirement, as long as they can work enough years, making reasonable wages.

Thus, employment is the real policy issue at hand. People who work most of their lives with a decent income have the luxury of planning for retirement. People who struggle to make a living wage most of their adult lives fall through the safety net and face poverty.

Key points:

Since its inception, Social Security's controversy has been a matter of effectively communicating the MODEL of its purpose. Social Security is neither "welfare" nor a retirement plan. It is a self-supporting social safety net. It is a wealth transfer program (the money you pay in is gone).

The demographic challenge for social security is not that people are living longer. The problem is that there are fewer people paying-in payroll taxes for each person collecting benefits.

For a program intended to keep people from falling into poverty, the benefits are more generous than necessary.

To preserve Social Security, Congress has options, each of which brings pain to taxpayers or beneficiaries:
- Increase payroll tax rates
- Increase income subject to payroll tax
- Increase taxation of social security benefits
- Extend the full retirement age
- Reduce the bend points used for calculating PIA
- Make the benefit base and contribution base different numbers

- Reduce benefits for retirees (perhaps based on need, or guarantee an income tied to the poverty level)

(Take a few minutes to think about it. Perhaps you can come up with better ideas.)

III. How People Get Used

Where we apply the Opinion-Framework to recognize how people get used. Users can be benign or malevolent. They touch and twist our beliefs about our world and ourselves. We should be aware of – and not OK with – getting used.

Applying the Framework

When we get used, we have something someone wants. They want our time, attention, money, votes, loyalty, buying preferences, trust, etc.

The Opinion-Framework can help you understand how people are getting used. Recall that opinion-beliefs are supported by a collection of belief-statements that can be categorized into Data, Models, and Values.

Let's start with OPINIONS. When we get used, both external and internal opinions are involved. This duality is the subtlety to getting used. In a disagreement, the debate involves your "external" opinions about topics like politics or your everyday life or your job. When you are getting used, those external opinions are still in play, but your "internal" opinions about yourself are also targeted. Internal opinions are tied to self-esteem beliefs. When we are used, we may question whether we are worthy or qualified in our roles as employees, friends, lovers, and parents.

When we get used, we cannot trust the DATA or the mental MODELS that users want us to accept. Users are willing to lie, or at least be selective, about data. They present only what supports their objectives. Users will also employ flawed logic and cognitive bias to manipulate our mental models.

When we are getting used, our VALUES are often under attack. Humans have deep needs to be right, to belong and be affiliated, to have meaning, and to be winners. We are quick to take offense when family or our work are criticized. We want to know that we are special and chosen, that we have access to secret knowledge. Users are clever at manipulating our values to get what they want.

Being used can be comfortable. It takes effort to think for yourself and respond to getting used. Yet, that effort is the price of freedom. Otherwise, employers will have you believe that it is too risky to find another job. Advertisers will convince you that you really need their products. Influencers will mislead you. People with power will manipulate you.

We all get used. It can be empowering to push back.

Key points:
- The Opinion-Framework applies as well to our opinions about ourselves as it does to opinions about the world we live in.
- When we are in a disagreement, it is usually obvious. Getting used can be subtle. We need to train ourselves to be more aware of our being used.

Power

Traditional sources of power can be formal or informal. Formal power comes from holding a position that has explicit authority: CEO, teacher, project manager, elected official, judge, trivia-night team leader. Informal power comes from personal attributes such as expertise, personality, an air of confidence, and interpersonal skills. To acquire informal power, it helps to be able to attract talent, generate sales, and get projects approved.

Let's focus on one example of acquiring and losing power.

Birth of McCarthyism

In the early 1950s, Senator Joseph McCarthy acquired a level of power out of proportion to his abilities or effectiveness. Elected in 1946 in a campaign filled with anti-communist rhetoric, McCarthy's career was ineffectual until 1950. There was a tradition of Republicans giving speeches to celebrate Lincoln's birthday. So, in February 1950, McCarthy spoke to a Republican Women's Club in Wheeling, WV. February 9th must have been a slow news day, because his speech made national headlines.

Two turns of phrase became famous: "enemies from within" and "I have here in my hand..." Here is a summary of the speech using the Opinion-Framework.

Enemies from Within Speech
OPINION
There are known traitors in the State Department who must be removed immediately.

DATA
Five years after a World War, we are not in a time of peace. We are in a "Cold War." There is an armaments race between two hostile camps.

The US is losing the Cold War. In six years, the number of people living within the Soviet orbit grew from 180 million to 800 million people.

Stalin has stated clearly that Communism cannot exist within a Christian democracy.

There are no soldiers invading our shores. Instead, traitors exist in our government - notably in the State Department. These traitors come from the privileged class of educated elites.

The Secretary of State has shown loyalty to a man guilty of treason.

"I have here in my hand … a list of names that were made known to the Secretary of State as being members of the Communist Party and who nonetheless are still working and shaping policy in the State Department…"

MODELS
There is a moral, not political, war being fought. A war between ideologies: that is, atheistic Marxism versus Christianity.

This ideology-based war is inevitable, because communism and democracy cannot coexist.

The threat is immediate, so we cannot wait or be complacent.

[Paraphrase attributed to Lincoln:] A great democracy is destroyed by "enemies from within."

The greatest threat we face in the Cold War is internal - traitors in government steering us to ruin.

VALUES
Peace/ Security
Christianity/ Belief in God
Anti-elitism
Trust (in government)

Senate Subcommittee on Investigations
McCarthy never shared the list. It was most likely a rehash of previous Loyalty Program investigations. Nevertheless, after his speech, McCarthy gained informal power and became a kingmaker within the Republican party. For three years, he campaigned on behalf of Republicans. He stayed in the news. He made many fiery accusations.

In 1953, Republicans gained a majority in the Senate. McCarthy was given formal power as chairman of the Senate Committee on Government Operations. By then, Senate leaders were leery of McCarthy's theatrics and hoped he would do the least harm there.

However, that committee included a Subcommittee on Investigations, which gave him the power to investigate and accuse government personnel and contractors. The subcommittee subpoenaed many witnesses, but none of McCarthy's investigations led to meaningful results.

Army-McCarthy hearings

In 1954, McCarthy's downfall began with some television news stories that were critical of him. McCarthy's committee had been investigating the Army. A member of McCarthy's staff was drafted by the Army. Bickering over how that draftee was treated snowballed into several weeks of televised hearings. For the first time, Americans watched prolonged sessions of McCarthy's behavior and methods.

There was a point where McCarthy began to drag the name of a former attorney for the Army into the mud. The Army's lead counsel then delivered the most memorable moment of weeks of testimony. He made an impassioned plea for McCarthy to stop bullying and ruining the reputation of the lawyer. Most dramatically, he seemed to be the first person to successfully pierce McCarthy's armor: "Senator, may we not drop this? We know he belonged to the Lawyers Guild ... Let us not assassinate this lad further, Senator; you've done enough. Have you no sense of decency, sir? At long last, have you left no sense of decency?"

Within months, the Senate condemned McCarthy and removed his chairmanship. Nonetheless, he continued his rhetoric for three years until he died while still in office.

Key points:
McCarthy was skilled at latching on to a hot political issue, violating norms of decorum, and ignoring facts. Throughout his years of popularity, McCarthy used exaggerations, untruths, threats, and accusations - but no one seemed to challenge him publicly, until the Army hearings.

He did well at gaining informal power. It is easy to be a critic and a gadfly. It is hard to run something and deliver real results. He stumbled when given formal power (with a limited scope). He lost the public's support as the hours of live broadcasts of the Army hearings exposed his methods.

What should not be lost in the drama of the McCarthy era is how easily Americans were willing to compromise (based on the rhetoric of one person) their core values of freedom, the rule of law, and civil rights.

Influence

Even benign influencers want something from us. They ask for contributions to support the causes they promote. They want your vote. They want you to buy their products and services. They want your loyalty. They want your time so that you generate advertising revenues. They say they care about us. We believe them.

Affiliations expect to have influence
We belong to various groups and organizations. Some have formal power and influence over us: employers, building co-ops, schools, our parents until we become adults. Some affiliations have informal power and influence: political parties, friends, hobbies and avocations, parents after we become adults and are in therapy. Affiliation groups have norms of behavior for members and may have beliefs and policies that members are expected to support.

Rogue thought leaders and influencers
Father Coughlin was an early radio personality who became a hate-promoting demagogue. At his most popular, about a third of American households regularly tuned in to his independently syndicated weekly broadcast.

He was a Catholic priest who started a weekly radio show in 1926 in Detroit to share Catholic teachings in response to KKK cross-burnings. In 1929, the new station owner encouraged Coughlin to shift from religious to political topics. In 1930, his show began to be broadcast nationally. Father Coughlin had rabid followers, zealous views, and raised enough money to build a new church and sustain his radio enterprise.

Over time his views became more hateful and targets of his attacks broadened. Father Coughlin hated usury (money lending) and the Federal Reserve. He blamed Jews and bankers for economic misery. He hated Communism as anti-Christian. He hated Capitalism as anti-worker. He supported and then turned against President Roosevelt. By 1936, he had embraced Fascism. In 1937, resistance to Coughlin began to build, until he was forced to stop his public life in 1942.

It was extraordinary that he could be so extreme for so long.

Instant Analysis is a harmful distraction

Watch for clickbait headlines that start with "Winners and losers in yesterday's …" Tough problems take time to understand and tackle. But influencers and news media must constantly generate content to keep their audiences engaged. So, they hound newsmakers and politicians nonstop for sound bites and results. Media engage in real-time analysis of uncertain events and complex policy discussions. Let's look at two examples: the NFL draft and Tax Reform.

NFL drafts have become entertainment. During the next pro football draft, watch for the "winners and losers" headlines. You should expect to see articles about yesterday's, or even today's, draft round. Don't be shocked to see an article cheeky enough to declare winners and losers in *tomorrow's* round.

It takes years to evaluate draft results. Historically, it is true that the best quarterbacks and running backs tend to be drafted in the first round (Tom Brady, Quarterback, Round 6, excepted). About half of the career receptions leaders have been drafted after the second round.

For the Year-2000 draft, the average career games-played by players drafted in rounds 1 through 3 turned out to be 97, while players drafted in rounds 4 to 7 averaged 59 games played. About 30% of the players on an NFL team's roster are undrafted. Perhaps trading early round picks for proven veterans or multiple picks in later rounds would be a good strategy.

If someone had written a winners and losers article in 1985 about a Senate Finance committee hearing for tax reform, the 1986 Tax Reform Act negotiations would have been a bumpy ride.

The 1986 Act was a bipartisan effort that took a couple of years to negotiate. The basic principle was to make the tax code fairer, simpler, and keep total revenues about the same.

The Act closed some loopholes and reduced the number of tax brackets, lowering the top bracket and raising the bottom. Long-term gains were taxed at ordinary rates. Standard deductions were increased.

These days, instant analysis and real-time comments by politicians on social media make it difficult to sustain long-term policy negotiations.

Advertising works or they wouldn't do it

We know that advertising is a price we pay for some content. Traditional ads interrupt what we are reading or watching. Display ads are more passive but still jarring. For example, NASCAR displays sponsor logos around the track, on the cars, and on the drivers' uniforms. Most product placement in print or video is more subtle than NASCAR.

While we may know an ad when we see it, the influence techniques underlying ads remain deeply effective. Ads are simple, because people have trouble making decisions when facing complexity. Ads that are focused on data (price or features) and pressure a buying decision work well in the short run. In the long run, ads that appeal to values (emotion, needs) create more brand loyalty.

One negative consequence of advertising is that it makes people unhappy. We have a sense that we are missing out or our lives aren't good enough.

Key points:
- Influence can be benign or harmful.
- It helps to be able to recognize influence techniques in action
- Influencers increasingly tend to be more extreme in their views and more instantaneous in their response to current events

Manipulation

An influencer gains support by reinforcing or gradually shifting people's opinions. A manipulator drives people toward actions that are not in their best interest. Manipulators distort truth. They attack people's emotions and values.

Magicians
Parents still invite magicians to children's birthday parties? We can see the appeal. If magic exists, then we can believe anything is possible no matter what our circumstances. Magicians offer a mild form of manipulation. They fool us into believing we see what we want to see.

Magic tricks use distraction, mirrors and secret compartments, the biology of human perception, and phrases and gestures that misdirect the audience's attention. The best approach to experiencing magic is to relax and allow yourself to be fooled without getting angry. Enjoy the sense of wonder.

There are two key magician skills that translate to getting used. First, distraction: deliver information overload, highlight irrelevant data, focus on unrelated cause and effect relationships. Second, secret knowledge: offer truths to which only a select few people are privy. Secret knowledge need not be logical or rational. Popular topics include conspiracies, supernatural powers, and hidden treasure. We want to be one of the "chosen" who know the truth.

Infotainment

Sensational news reporting and eye-catching headlines are not new. In the late 1800's, publishers Hearst and Pulitzer engaged in "yellow journalism" as their newspapers (the World and Journal) battled for market share in New York City.

Ad revenues increased with circulation. Circulation rose with lurid and flowery prose, that breathlessly told stories about crime and exposed corruption. These stories were accompanied by color images, comics, games, and longer articles. These newspapers weren't shy about using fake interviews, unnamed sources, and exaggerated headlines.

Later in life, Pulitzer shifted away from this tabloid-style journalism. He believed that journalistic independence and integrity were important. In his will, he funded the creation of the Columbia School of Journalism and the Pulitzer Prizes.

In 1968, a new style of broadcast news (branded as Eyewitness News) was begun at an ABC affiliate in New York City. That style influenced news reporting nationally. Until then, TV news consisted of a man, sitting at a desk, reading the news. He was replaced by anchor-hosts who would cut to reporters on-location to provide live reporting. The anchors had more energy than traditional news presenters. They would engage in unscripted banter that lightened up the show. The stories focused on crime, sensationalized versions of normal stories, and exposing misconduct of powerful people. If it bleeds it leads. Viewer market share soared. Unfortunately, exaggerating the news (especially, emphasizing crime) made viewers more fearful than they should have been.

Information Overload

Since 1980 - a series of technological advances has overwhelmed news consumers. First, cable tv offered more channels than broadcast tv. Then, all-news cable channels turned content into a commodity. Now, internet and cellular bandwidth have made streaming newsfeeds ubiquitous. Anyone with a smartphone can be a "journalist."

"Narrowcasting" of the news and personalized advertising have supported extremism. Now, it seems OK to lie. If you lie enough, the fact-checkers can't keep up. If Pulitzer were alive today, he might wonder how we are to encourage standards of excellence and integrity.

Liars

In normal discourse, liars must be convincing, but sooner or later, the truth catches up to them. However, there are two good ways for liars to dodge the burden of proof: avoid the truth or tell an alternate truth.

Avoidance takes many forms. Don't answer any direct questions. Instead, change the subject. Belittle opponents by making fun of their background and appearance. Obfuscate with strawman logic and lots of irrelevant facts. Use facial expressions, theatrical sighs, and steamrolling interruptions to distract listeners. Attack the person rather than the opinion. Find a small error or a misspoken phrase and claim that the opponent's whole argument must be rejected.

Alternative truths are a way of denying facts without proof. Subject matter experts can be hired to say nearly anything. Pile up enough lies and the fact checkers can't keep up. Dog whistles, stereotypes, and name-calling are shorthand forms of alternative truths.

Gaslighting is an extreme form of manipulative lying to control victims. The gaslighter gains trust and starts to push false information. Gaslighters limit a victim's contact with friends, family, and trusted sources of information to disconnect the victim from reality. If sustained, this lying causes a victim to question what they know to be true.

Key points:
- A combination of distraction and focused attention can make the human brain see things that aren't there.
- Sensationalizing information attracts and keeps an audience.
- Lying in media and social media is commonplace and has become normalized. Highly skilled liars can convince their followers of the validity of an alternate reality.
- Without an agreed-upon version of truth it is difficult to hold people accountable for their actions.

Subjugation

If influence is about shifting someone's opinion, and manipulation is about driving people to action, then subjugation is about domination and control. There are different types of subjugation. What they have in common is that the subjugator's source of control is within the victim. Subjugators take advantage of people's biases, prejudices, issues with self-esteem, and need for meaning.

Pimps
Pimps control their victims, treating them as if they are commodities. They tend to recruit people who are vulnerable, naïve, and lack confidence. Pimps take the time to listen to their victims. Grooming can take months. They promise money, stability, and anything the victim wants. Pimps enforce rules to control their victims, and they isolate their victims from friends, family, and anyone who can be supportive.

Pimps can be violent, threatening their victims or families of victims. They may trap their victims into drug use. Pimps don't always have to use violence or be scary. They may use leverage, such as explicit photos or a victim's criminal past, to coerce a victim into the sex business. Victims who are in the country illegally are trapped and can't trust the legal system.

Pimps may pretend to be in love with the victim. They may offer a business proposition to prospective victims by pretending to be agents. Along the way, pimps keep attacking a victim's self-esteem and dehumanizing them.

Propaganda

Propaganda can be directed at your supporters or your opponents. It serves to steer public opinion to a path that enables an agenda that can be positive or negative. Propaganda can take any form: posters, leaflets, books, tv, movies, news reports. Awareness of propaganda diminishes its power.

Effective propaganda is simple, well-timed, and repetitive. It uses loaded language that connects negatively to stereotypes and prejudice and connects positively to patriotism, honor, and self-sacrifice. Data and logic are used sparingly. Telling the truth or lies is a matter of choosing what will work best. Propaganda primarily appeals to our core values and emotions.

Normally, we do not want to hurt people or take away their human rights. However, when we are affected by propaganda that dehumanizes our opponents (for example, calling them "vermin"), it becomes acceptable to imprison or exterminate them.

Propaganda is thousands of years old and ubiquitous today. Autocrats are especially fond of propaganda. Nation-states and extremists are actively trying to undermine America and democracy.

Social Constructs

Social constructs are things or categories that are not real in objective reality but are real when people agree that they are so. Social constructs are useful. They help humans acquire knowledge, enable us to live and work together, and place guard rails on our behavior.

Social constructs are pervasive:

Category	Social Construct Examples
Identity	Gender roles, race, ethnicity, social class, nationality, country boundaries
Interactions	Language, roles in family or community
Social norms	Manners, fashion, social class, beauty standards, taboos and sources of shame
Philosophy	Religion, myths, intelligence, education, human rights
Commerce	Money, law and order, contractual commitments, property ownership
Affiliation	Patriotism, culture, marriage, family

Social constructs are a way to control people and help powerful people to hold on to their power. Complex societies and cultures have countless social constructs.

How do social constructs relate to the Opinion-Framework? They are the main drivers of opinions and supporting belief statements. They are usually the basis for what we call facts and data. They affect our cause-and-effect mental models. Lastly, social constructs are the primary source of our values.

Key points:
- Controlling people is possible when you make them feel trapped and attack their self-esteem.
- Blaming and dehumanizing people makes it easier to justify treating them unfairly.
- Propaganda does not make people hate. Instead, propaganda cultivates the seeds of hatred that are already present in the audience.
- Social constructs make it possible to distort people's reality.

Case Study: Outrage

A clickable headline you could have read during the pandemic: "Kids Take Stolen Kia for a Joyride - Injuries Reported"

How does that headline make you feel?
Let's review some of the ways that you might feel "outraged" by this story. In other words, let's see how many reasons an algorithm might put this story at the top of your newsfeed.

This type of car theft is a crime that threatens your sense of security. It could happen near you - at home, work, shopping - not in some sketchy urban neighborhood. Thieves stole these cars for fun, and to use as battering rams for entering a store.

The thieves stealing cars are often minors, some even too young to have a driver's license. They are reckless and don't care about hurting others. As minors, they won't be prosecuted as adults.

As if pandemic-related school closures weren't disrupting our lives enough, it seemed that these kids were probably unsupervised and bored – you might believe that these joyrides provide evidence that remote learning doesn't work.

Outrage does not mean what it used to

Are we really *outraged* by the Kia theft stories? Moral outrage was a term reserved for the most egregious violations of social norms (rape, torture, senseless killings).

The act was the "outrage." Now, the emotion felt by the person who learns of an act is the "outrage." Over-usage of the term has diluted its import. People are now expected to be outraged at sporting fans who misbehave. Put the word, outrage, in a headline, and you will get more clicks.

DATA: Car theft trends

For thirty years after 1990, car theft rates dropped. Auto theft investigators became more effective at catching and prosecuting car theft. Cars were built with better anti-theft technology, and smart keys made new cars impossible to hot-wire.

US Auto Theft Rate History

Year	Theft Rate per 100k persons
1990	658
2000	412
2010	245
/	/
2019	221
2020	247
2021	256
2022	283

Source: Federal Bureau of Investigation

Notice the upswing from 2019 to 2022. The first half of that increase was due to auto thefts by tech-savvy thieves targeting opportunities during the pandemic lockdown. Their methods require hacking the computer network in cars, cloning wireless key codes and fob signals. But in 2021 and 2022, low-tech thefts of Kias and Hyundais skyrocketed.

MODEL 1: Blame Kia and Hyundai

Unlike most manufacturers, Kia and Hyundai, for about ten years prior to 2021, opted not to install car immobilizers. The Kia/ Hyundai theft technique is not technical. Thieves break into the car, remove the cover on the steering column, dismantle the ignition cylinder, then use a USB-A connector (that happens to be a perfect fit) to physically turn on the ignition.

Without an immobilizer, the vehicle can be driven if you can bypass the ignition and get the car started. For years, these vulnerable cars were waiting to be easily stolen. What triggered the USB-hack crime wave?

MODEL 2: Blame Social Media

The viral popularity of the USB hack is commonly reported to have begun in Milwaukee, in 2021. As part of a social media challenge, a group of car thieves posted videos of themselves wearing masks, stealing cars, and going for joyrides. The number of cars stolen nearly tripled in that city, and nearly all of that growth in thefts were Kia and Hyundai models. By the summer of 2022, the trend spread to varying degrees to other cities. So, the jump in theft rate from 2021 to

2022 can be explained by more Kias and Hyundais being stolen by more juveniles.

MODEL 3: Blame Algorithms

Kia and Hyundai received heavy doses of vitriol, partly due to algorithms and social media. Algorithms fed viral how-to-steal videos to receptive audiences (potential thieves). Then, algorithms fed news stories about car thefts to receptive audiences (nervous car owners). That cycle repeated itself and outrage ensued.

In the frenzy, State Attorney's General responded by filing lawsuits against Kia and Hyundai. The car manufacturers made some overdue software updates and a hardware fix for the ignition cylinder to counter the theft technique.

VALUES: Negativity Bias deserves the blame

Emotional content that involves threats to our values is more likely to be passed on to people in our networks. Content that criticizes opponents is more viral than content that supports us.

It was reported that changes to an algorithm in Facebook meant to increase positive and healthy interactions among friends and family unexpectedly rewarded negativity, exaggeration, and anger.

Some studies have shown that we tend to overestimate how angry social media posters are. We pay attention to critical and negative tweets. On the other hand, we are more accurate in estimating the happiness of positive posters. This negativity bias causes downward spirals within online communities, where people are generating and sharing content that tends to reinforce outrage.

Social media and algorithms may be enablers, but negativity bias is the third leg of the stool that supports outrage-based search results and media feeds. This bias is a human trait that energizes gossip – and it has been around since we invented language.

Key points:
- Outrage is an emotional response to behavior that violates social norms
- Algorithms exploit our negativity bias, leading us to click and share negative information more readily than positive

Case Study: Health Care

Why is Health Care a means of Subjugation?
We can calmly discuss rationing health care, until it becomes personal. When a family member is sick, cost is no object. In healthcare, unlike other industries, we are trapped by our core values and a complex system with misaligned incentives.

The Hippocratic oath was a commitment by healers to do what they can to help a patient and not to do harm. For more than two thousand years, healers have wanted to do what they can to cure and relieve suffering. Health care was low-cost and somewhat effective. Healing had an aura of magic and miracles.

For the past hundred years, healers have been able to do increasingly more to help their patients. Advances in germ theory, antibiotics, anesthesia, surgery, and pharmaceuticals made "cures" a reality. Now, we have powers to heal that used to belong to the gods. But at what cost?

Today, as a matter of policy, whenever we can cure illnesses and relieve suffering, we feel we must do so. Hospital emergency departments that get government money must screen and treat patients regardless of their ability to pay. We are unable to resolve the conflict between the aspirations of the health care industry and budget constraints.

DATA: Health Care Expenditures

Health care costs in the US as a % of GDP

Year	% of GDP
1960	5.0%
1970	6.9%
1980	8.9%
1990	12.1%
2000	13.3%
2010	17.2%
2020	19.7%

Source: Preeti Vankar, U.S. health expenditure as percent of GDP 1960-2022, Statista.com

Note: Health care costs in the US as a percentage of GDP is now more than three times the spending on Food (5%).

Spending per person on health care in the US is about twice that of comparable countries. Most of the higher costs in the US are due to higher operating costs, medication costs, and doctor wages. It does not appear to be the case that people in the US visit the doctor, or go to hospitals, more often than in comparable countries.

For consumer household expenditures, Food is about 13% of annual spending, while Health insurance/ care is about 8%. If GDP health spending is much greater than food, yet consumer spending on health is less than food, where does that money come from? Answer: employers and governments are subsidizing health care costs.

DATA: Health Care Effectiveness

Many factors affect health, including lifestyle, diet, and compliance with medical advice. So, it can be difficult to assess the effectiveness of health care in the US compared to other countries. However, it appears that the US is slightly less effective than comparable countries (e.g., UK, Japan, Canada, several European nations). In rankings of quality of care and level of satisfaction, the US is middling.

In 1980, the US and comparable countries had similar life expectancies (about 74 years). By 2019, the US improved to 79 while comparable countries reached close to 83 years. Pregnancy mortality rates are surprising: in 2020, the maternal mortality rate (deaths per 100,000 live births) was about 24 for the US and 4 for comparable countries. Hospital admission rates (per 100,000 population) for the chronic conditions of congestive heart failure and diabetes were twice as high for the US versus comparable countries.

MODELS: Players and Incentives

Health Insurance is a misnomer. It is not "insurance" in the same way that auto insurance works. Auto insurance premiums are pooled to help people pay for events that are low probability but high cost (serious accidents, injuries, lawsuits). Auto insurance does not pay for maintenance (oil changes, brake pads, or new transmissions).

Health insurance is really a form of health care *financing*. Health Care Providers (doctors, hospitals) set high list prices. Payers (insurance companies and governments) negotiate substantial discounts (75% in many cases) and pay for most of the service costs. Employers who offer health care benefits pay most of the insurance premiums due the Payers. Subscribers (patients) pay a share of the insurance premiums, plus deductibles and co-pays when receiving care.

The issue is the tension among the players at balancing the level of care with the costs. If doctors want to do more, and patients don't experience all the costs, then costs go up for marginally better results.

Player	Roles and Incentive Misalignment
Providers	Expected to provide care even for patients who cannot pay Charge high prices to compensate for high capital and operating costs Have incentives to provide more tests and treatments per patient
Insurers/Payers	Manage risks by pooling beneficiaries into large groups Negotiate rates with providers Bear most of the costs of care Have a high desire to reduce costs, encourage preventive care, challenge diagnoses, and ration care
Employers	May offer health insurance as part of employee compensation Indirect desire to reduce costs (premiums are the same per

Player	Roles and Incentive Misalignment
	employee, regardless of how much care an employee receives)
Subscribers/ Patients	Tend to be very price sensitive. But they see only part of the total cost of care. So, they have a weaker desire to reduce costs and a very strong aversion to ration care
	Often make unhealthy choices
	When ill, they have a high desire to pursue tests and treatments, even if expensive or experimental

VALUES: Ethics and health policy

Some people believe that medical care is a human right. Which begs the question as to whether other spending categories should be human rights: food, shelter, and transportation.

The ethical challenge is how to ration care, not overtreat, and focus on quality of life as people age or are experiencing end-of-life illnesses. Is it ethical for income or wealth to enable a higher quality of care? To what extent should Payers have a say in the level of care to provide?

Key points:

- US health care is high-cost but with middling outcomes compared to peer countries
- Attempts to reform health care end up being reforms to health care *financing*
- Rational health care policy is very difficult to achieve

Case Study: The American Dream

When founded, America offered a promise – the land of opportunity. The American Dream began as a commitment to make good on that promise – give everyone opportunity regardless of social class. Over time, the American Dream evolved to be a promise of material success to everyone.

The American Promise came first
Let's distinguish the American Promise from the American Dream. A promise is a guarantee. A dream is an aspiration.

The American Promise focuses on the individual being able to pursue "happiness" – not meaning "elation" but, rather, living well in concert with nature and government. Morality and virtue are key qualities in practicing this kind of happiness.

Colonial America claimed to promise freedom, opportunity, and escape from persecution to everyone. More recently, civil rights and antiwar movements reaffirmed that the ideal of the American Promise should be available to all.

History of the American Dream
The American Dream gained traction in the early 1900s. It was an affirmation that we should offer

everyone the chance to pursue success. Democracy was promoted as the enabler of success. Greed and excess wealth were seen as hindering equality.

Before the market crash in 1929, some supporters of Hoover's presidential campaign ran an ad touting the prosperity that Republicans had delivered in the 1920s ("A chicken in every pot…"). The American Dream had shifted from living in a society that enables the pursuit of success to living a life that actually achieves success.

By the 1950s, the Dream became more materialistic. You needed to own a car, own a home with many appliances, send kids to college, and go on family vacations. By 1970, a comfortable and secure retirement became part of the American Dream. Later in the 20th century, "greed is good" promoted an aspiration of limitless wealth.

Current State of the American Dream

Materialism within the American Dream is a form of subjugation. The American Dream is now boundless in a way that worsens income inequality. In religion, there are churches that preach the "Prosperity Gospel." If you have faith, God will give you what you want in this life: money, good health, family. Failing to be prosperous and successful might be evidence that your faith is wanting.

There are two challenges in the materialistic American Dream: making enough money to pay the bills while you are working and saving enough money to live a life of leisure in retirement.

When things are going well, wage earners in the average consumer household can meet normal expenses. Unfortunately, the Dream costs more than normal expenses. For decades, the cost of putting kids through college has grown faster than real income. Owning a home has always been a financial challenge. When misfortune, illness, or accidents happen, the pursuit of the American Dream is further derailed for many families who are otherwise on track.

The notion that retirement is a good thing is a 20th century invention. Previously, most workers kept working as long as they could. When they stopped working, they depended on family or charities if they didn't have sources of income. Today, for a majority of Americans, retirement can be a scary financial prospect. Many people want to, or need to, work beyond retirement age.

The American Promise can be offerable to every American. With equal rights, equal opportunity, and hard work, you have the opportunity to build a better life for you and your family. America can provide freedom and a sense of belonging to everyone.

The American Dream seems possible for less than half of Americans. Trouble is, people who are below middle income, have been unemployed, have had chronic health issues, or must be care providers for family members miss out on the Dream.

We can guarantee opportunity (the Promise). We cannot guarantee results (the Dream). People who are not on track for the idealized American Dream that we see in ads and on social media feel left out and disillusioned. They are likely to distrust government, search for someone to blame, lose faith in democracy, and embrace extremism.

Options for the Future of the American Dream

The fundamental ethical question is: how many Americans should we expect will achieve the American Dream? Is it OK for only some people to make it? After all, the Dream is not a promise. It is an "aspiration." Aspirations don't come with a guarantee. Most childhood dreams are out of reach: NBA player, principal ballet dancer, astronaut, rock star, movie star. We tell children to dream big. We tend to discourage adults who dream big.

The key issue is that we sell the American Dream to adults as being feasible for everyone. Political policy rhetoric and advertisements for consumer products and services frame the Dream as if it is a right.

So, what's to be done? To encourage a range of thinking, here are a few perspectives. Spend a few minutes pondering the American Dream. What would we be like as a country with a better path to the Dream, or a reframed Dream?

Opinion	Implied Data, Models, and Values
Stay the Course - use innovation to make the Dream feasible for all	Data and Models: America is designed for prosperity. There are ways to make home ownership, college, retirement, and "materialism" more affordable. People need tangible goals in life. If we focus on productivity and efficiency, leverage artificial intelligence, develop clean/ abundant energy, then we can

Opinion	Implied Data, Models, and Values
	provide enough for all with the smaller workforce of the future. Related Values: freedom, creativity, trust in capitalism, invest in the future
Stop selling the Dream and return to the Promise	Data and Models: Technology revolutions made people more productive, which helped create the middle class and the modern American Dream. We have gone too far, and the Dream is bloated. The federal debt is a piper that must be paid. We need smaller government and a freer economy. We should redesign social security to be a simple safety net payment and not a retirement plan. Shift the bend points, or add a new one, to make benefits more needs-based. Manage health care expectations/ costs, and reward healthy behaviors. Stop subsidizing home ownership. Challenge the value of four-year colleges and promote ongoing adult learning, so that people can renew their skills and pursue new career dreams. Related Values: self-reliance, competition, private business incentives
Rewire our thinking about Success	Data and Models: Humans are never satisfied. Our ancestors dreamed of being warm in the winter and having plenty to eat. Today, we have central heating, air conditioning, and grocery

Opinion	Implied Data, Models, and Values
	stores. But we're not happy. We have had an industrial revolution and an IT revolution.
	We need an enlightenment revolution. We should teach gratitude and an appreciation for living well versus a higher standard of living.
	Related Values: cooperation, environmentalism, gratitude

Key points:
- America's Promise should not be confused with the American Dream
- People who feel that the Dream is beyond their grasp are likely to feel disillusioned and embrace influencers with flawed opinions
- Resetting the American Psyche may be needed to rein in the American Dream

IV. What is to be Done?

Where we walk through a way to set ourselves up for success when tackling a difficult problem. We combine the Opinion-Framework with some generic problem-solving steps to help make our projects well-scoped and feasible. It is reassuring to know that when we are thinking for ourselves about a problem that matters to us, there are practical actions we can pursue that will make a difference. It is not enough to have opinions and voice complaints. We must not hesitate to act. Our actions, big or small, are worthy.

Leverage the Framework

People make problems worse

When a group of people have a shared vision and pull together, they can solve tough problems. When there are differences of opinion and incentives are misaligned, positive change is tough to achieve.

This part of the book dovetails elements of the Opinion-Framework with a generic approach to problem-solving. Don't overthink the problem-solving steps. They are a collection of conscious decisions that will help you tackle the people-issues that cause trouble when you work a plan. The next five chapters explore each problem-solving step in turn.

Problem-Solving Step	How each Step is supported by the Opinion-Framework
Define the problem and why you care	Focus on Data and research needed
Know why you have a right to succeed	Evaluate existing mental Models, and consider alternative Models
Focus on key leverage points to target	Look for conflicting Values that can be the source of persistent disagreements

Problem-Solving Step	How each Step is supported by the Opinion-Framework
Choose the tools and methods to use	Plan to harness power and influence to counter Getting Used
Start	Confirm that Opinions about yourself align with your intent to make a difference

What drives interpersonal conflict?

To diagnose an opinion in real-life situations using the Opinion-Framework, just listen. Hear how people justify their opinions. Categorize those supporting belief-statements into data, models, and values. Don't worry about capturing everything that they say. Listen for where the energy and emotion come through.

Descriptions of symptoms mean that the opinion is data-driven. When you hear an emphasis on process, then the opinion is models-driven. Heavy emotion, righteousness, and a reliance on some external authority means the opinion is values-driven.

Conflict, disagreements, and getting used happen when two or more parties have a persistent misalignment of supporting belief-statements. Misalignment of beliefs can occur within a category (data, models, or values) or across categories. For example, one person may be data-driven while their opponent is values-driven. The most intractable disagreements happen when people have different core values.

In most situations, tackling disagreements and pushing back at getting used are not worth the effort.

However, there are times when you are committed to getting things done and must face the challenges of disagreements and getting used.

Let's practice on a few scenarios

Three scenarios are carried through each of the next four chapters to show how to practically apply these methods. These scenarios are meant to illustrate personal, work, and policy situations that touch on a range of Opinion-Framework elements covered in this book.

Personal Scenario: Fringe Beliefs

Problem	A friend has recently adopted some wacky beliefs
Contributing Conditions	Newsfeeds manipulate readers with sensational clickbait. Influencers spread harmful misinformation. Technology helps fringe-thinking achieve scale.
Key Framework Elements	Lies, deceit, manipulation, deep value issues

At Work Scenario: Inventory Project

Problem	Your boss assigns you to lead a project to reduce in-process and finished goods inventories.
Contributing Conditions	Inventory issues can be difficult to diagnose. They often lead to a misguided IT project. At work, you may need to counteract power-grabs

	and factions. This project could end your career.
Key Framework Elements	Power, flawed mental models, resistance to change, needs-based values (being right, in control)

Policy Issue Scenario: Homelessness

Problem	You want to make a real difference, but what can one person do?
Contributing Conditions	On the surface, homelessness seems simple and visible - people living on the streets and in city parks. Less visible are people one paycheck or act of violence away from becoming homeless. There are a range of homelessness causes, so simple solutions usually fail and often generate unintended consequences.
Key Framework Elements	Quality of available data, non-aligned mental models, conflicting core values (human rights, charity, equality)

Key points:

In this part of the book, it seems that we have gone overboard with the frameworks! We are mashing up three things – just go with it:
- The Opinion-Framework.
- A five-step problem-solving process. One step per chapter.
- Three illustrative scenarios. To make the dry content of this book more palatable.

Define the Problem and Why You Care

Define the problem
This design choice is critical to success. Be clear on the boundaries of the scope of the problem. Describe the problem without stating the solution. Can the problem be measured in a way that proves a solution is working?

Decide if the problem is worth solving. There may be other priorities for you or your organization. Stakeholders and sponsors should be willing to champion a solution.

Know why you care
Some problems are challenging and will take a lot of your time and energy. If you have the latitude and discretionary authority, decide if you are motivated enough to do the work. It can be a long, frustrating haul.

When assessing the scope, start thinking about the scale at which you will address the problem. Big organizations and big teams usually tackle big problems. However, there may be leverage points for individuals and small teams to target and make a significant impact on big challenges.

Scenarios
Fringe Beliefs.

Don't confront, argue, make fun of, or try to prove your friend is wrong. Listen to him talk. Categorize his supporting beliefs into Data, Models, and Values. Ask where he gets information and how long he has been thinking along these lines. Ask how much time your friend spends per day viewing content or engaging with like-minded people.

Inventories.

Bummer. You should have been on vacation when your boss gave out this assignment. She said, "We have to decrease inventories. Get a team together and come up with a plan." You'd better get your arms around the impetus for the assignment and the opinions at play.

You might want to find out who brought up this problem, what data is there, what is a "good" level of inventory, what changed to make this an urgent issue, what function on the organization chart "owns" inventory, how sales and operations coordinate, etc. At this stage, you should not feel relaxed.

Homelessness.

Homelessness is a collection of problems, not a single problem. You should expect that solutions will have to be designed to match local conditions. It would be a mistake to look for quick answers.

Learn the terminology of homeless advocacy: sheltered vs unsheltered, temporary vs permanent housing, housing cost burden (rent as a percentage of income). Look at data to see how close to being homeless many people are. Living paycheck to paycheck means any unexpected expense or loss of a job tips the scale.

Key points:
- If you don't internalize the problem, then you won't have the motivation needed to sustain the work and make an impact
- It is critical to define a problem carefully. Be specific about the symptoms. Avoid assuming up front what the answer is. Know how to measure what success looks like.

Know Why You Have a Right to Succeed

Situational awareness
When it comes to policy issues, pay attention to how special interests are trying to influence and use you. Politicians love your vote, not you. Advertisers love you only if you buy things. You are of value if you spend money on subscriptions, products, or write reviews and tell your friends about what you buy.

In work or personal situations, learn the lay of the land. Diagnose any disagreements, politics, resource constraints, and non-alignment of philosophy among stakeholders. Make the rounds. Talk to people. Learn how and why people who have done work like yours in the past have tried and failed. Capture opinions and their supporting data, models, and values beliefs. See what you are up against and where power resides.

Discover resources
Powerful people fear an informed electorate. Voting used to be limited to white male property owners. Gradually, voting rights were extended. The history of enfranchisement and disenfranchisement is appalling.

Organizations respect consumer power. Boycotts were a way to force change, and they still work. But consumer power has expanded to online reviews and influence that can have a greater impact on consumer behavior than traditional advertising.

Harness power

As a consumer, you can get paid to surf the web. You can promote products and services via your social media interactions. You can write reviews and comments that will have an impact on businesses.

As an employee, you should learn how to navigate the annual funding process. The budget game can be a full-contact sport. Some of the best fiction you'll read is in the strategic plans of business units looking for approval of capital projects, acquisitions, and research and development investments. Small companies, especially those run by founders, need people who can weave a compelling story for investors.

As a policy champion, you can help non-profit organizations compete for grants. There are billions of dollars available each year. There are tens of thousands of grantmaking entities. Some are government programs, especially in health care.

As a voter, you can make a difference on a local level by enabling people to register and vote. Currently, younger voters tend to favor Democrats and older persons favor Republicans. Thirty years ago, that age-based difference was less significant. Older persons are more likely to be registered and vote, but all age groups have substantial numbers of eligible, unregistered people.

Census data shows that there is an opportunity for those who can deliver votes. In the table, notice how the under-24 population had only 56% registered (and about 8% of that 56% did not vote). Given how many elections are decided by narrow margins, the means to increase turnout is a goldmine.

2020 Voting Turnout by Age Group
Population in (000s)

Age Group	Population	% Registered	% Voted
18 to 24	28,659	56%	48%
25 to 44	86,429	62%	55%
45 to 64	81,912	70%	66%
65 and older	55,273	76%	72%

Source: census.gov

Scenarios

Fringe Beliefs.
Verify that your friend is sincere in his beliefs. Promoting fringe beliefs can be a form of attention-seeking or protest against the establishment. Does he have just one fringe belief or a collection - which would indicate core values (like a need to be right or to belong) are at stake.

Define success - do you hope to change his mind or give him mental space to change himself? Does he see you, or anyone who does not share his beliefs, as an adversary?

Inventories.
Interview stakeholders in the company to gauge how much enthusiasm or power they have to help make the

project a success. Find out how success is measured. There should be a clear understanding of what causes inventory levels and how inventory helps to debottleneck operations or meet customer needs.

Check if senior leaders are simply unhappy with the inventory expense numbers that are on the income statement. If so, then your project needs to start with an education phase for leaders, so everyone has a shared understanding of the problem.

Is there money set aside to run the project and pay for capital and expenses for implementation? If you hear the phrase "IT Project," then things are going to get rough for you.

Homelessness.
Identify the major stakeholders in your community, such as government agencies, nonprofits, thinktanks, charities, housing market experts, law enforcement, and homeless advocates.

What specific role do you want to play? What is the scope of that role and what outcomes do you aspire to achieve? To avoid being discouraged, you will have to set modest goals and be realistic about the impact you can have - yet you must not give up.

Key points:
- It is hard to renegotiate the scope of a project after it has been running
- Do everything you can to design the work so that you will succeed. Push the risky and costly activities into a later phase

Focus on Key Leverage Points to Target

Cattle drives in the 19th and early 20th century are part of American cowboy lore. While massive cattle herds were being driven to slaughterhouses out West, back East the timber industry had lesser-known *log* drives. Huge log flotillas were driven down-river to sawmills, with men riding atop logs rather than horses.

Dangerous work. A logjam might cover acres. Log drivers would carefully, but quickly, pick away at a jam, using a peavey pole. It took courage and a practical sense of physics to hop about the island of logs – choosing just the right ones to dislodge – freeing hundreds of trapped logs.

In situations where there are disagreements and people are getting used, a logjam-mindset will help you focus your efforts. Not as dangerous as standing on a log in the middle of a river, but it is risky. Find the handful of people and ideas in the organization who are clogging the works. By carefully choosing where to target your efforts, you can have a significant impact picking apart problems of any size. So, where to start?

Muddled thinking
When someone is supporting an opinion with data belief-statements, watch for tricky statistics. For example,

- Big changes in small numbers may not matter.
- Drawing big conclusions from small samples.
- One outlier does not disprove a trend.
- Look at charts and graphs carefully to see if the scale on the axis is too clever.
- Correlation does not mean causation.
- As always, keep in mind that the 80/20 rule should not be surprising.

Roots of lies and propaganda

In a community or organization, identify people who are sharing misinformation. Trace back to identify their data source. Fact-checking does not seem to work on those who originate lies and errors. However, calling out lies and sloppy sharing of content may help to throttle down the flow of misinformation passed on by unwitting followers.

Policy principles

There are unintended consequences for most simplistic policies. Health care costs management, crime prevention, fixing social security, and deficit reduction are examples of complex initiatives. Find and challenge the underlying principles within policy debates. Watch for the language people use, such as the health care reform vs. health care *financing* reform.

In some cases, Policy is subjugation. Target situations where civil rights are threatened. Politicians are remarkably transparent at voter suppression.

Power

Two big targets to leverage when it comes to power: Hypocrisy and corruption.

Whenever possible, catch the hypocrites *not* doing as they say. Preachers commit adultery. Parents falsify information in their kid's school applications. Pro-life advocates escort a relative out of state to get an abortion. All-natural fitness advocates take anabolic steroids.

Corruption is rampant. White-collar crime costs hundreds of billions of dollars per year. On the other hand, street crimes (like burglary, larceny and theft that make news headlines) cost just tens of billions. Nonetheless, sentencing for non-violent crimes is lighter than for violent crimes.

Prosecution of white-collar crimes is tricky, because you must prove "intent." Defendants will claim ignorance of the law or that their actions were "business as usual." So, probation and fines are more likely than prison.

Your best bet for a criminal case for corruption is to catch someone committing fraud or embezzlement. Intent is clear. Otherwise, for corruption such as bribery, lucrative contracts for cronies, and bending rules, the best we can do might be to expose and shame the perpetrators as an alternative to going to court.

Secret knowledge

Humans have a deep need for meaning and feeling special. Secret knowledge feeds that need and may be the most important leverage point for you to target.

Secret knowledge supports conspiracy theories, extremism, unregulated investments, fad diets, and deep distrust of authority and science.

Often, providers of secret knowledge lure people into a community to be fleeced. You'll know it when you see it:
- Evidence of a "deep state."
- How to get to heaven.
- How to be rich and successful on earth if your faith is strong enough and you pay a hefty fee.
- Ponzi schemes and insider trading.

Scenarios
Fringe Beliefs.

Identify problems that these fringe beliefs address for your friend. The fringe beliefs might be a symptom of deeper, triggering issues. For example, if your friend has money problems, then blaming immigrants or the government helps him to believe that his problems are not his fault.

Meanwhile, identify any gaps in his logic. Challenge the source of his beliefs, by highlighting other views espoused by his thought leader that your friend may not agree with. Repeatedly say things that let him know that it is okay, even admirable, to change one's mind.

Inventories.

Figure out how to address any sponsorship issues for inventory. An executive must have some authority over the drivers of inventory. Try to ensure that the leader of inventory management has some clout.

Consider bringing in external consultants. Experts can help elevate your project's importance. Let people know that there are some key skills required to be good at inventory management.

Homelessness.
Scan the policy landscape. There are many causes of homelessness. Identify opportunities to use existing resources like the following:

Causes Of homelessness	Resources that can be leveraged
High Rent	Tax base, urban vs suburban, zoning, project pipeline
Low Income	Subsidies, transition housing
Unemployment	Identify at-risk individuals early
Domestic Violence	Rapid response interim housing, childcare
Mental Health and addiction	Outreach, medication distribution
Jail Crowding	Alternative hospitalization
Being Unsheltered	Food banks, temporary beds

Key points:
- Borrow power and credibility whenever you can
- Watch for lies and secret knowledge. These people believe that they are above the law

Choose the Tools and Methods to Use

Some logjams are good. You can restore stream health and fish habitat by placing logs and other sturdy debris in key locations in a stream bed. These logjams slow down the flow of water and provide a refuge for fish.

With common sense and a few influence tools, you can put in place beneficial logjams. Be the person in online communities who impacts thought leaders. At work, be the person people ask to sanity-check project plans. Be the person on social media who calms the latest viral frenzy. Be the person at home who takes care of family and friends by pointing out scams and "too good to be true" sales pitches. Here are some log-jamming techniques.

Follow the money and watch your wallet

When wealthy and powerful people spend money, they expect something in return. Find campaign funding data and see who is behind political action committees that are active in areas of interest to you. Learn why advertisers keep spending money to reach you. Look at where products are manufactured and assembled. Check on the sources of funding for research that supports weight loss drugs and nutritional supplements. And, for goodness' sake, think twice before investing in funds with high fees and front-end, or back-end, loads.

Illuminate flawed thinking

Most of us never use calculus or geometry in our adult lives. On the other hand, we need to be good at personal finance, statistics, and data visualization. Consider working with your local school district to provide more useful math in school curriculums or direct students to supplemental learning opportunities.

If a medical test is known to have a relatively high false positive rate, then you shouldn't get the test unless you meet screening criteria.

The 80/20 rule can help to explain what we see, such as when a crime spree is due to a small number of perpetrators.

Start looking more closely at data and charts you find in news articles. There are some good books that explain how people lie, or at least skew the truth, by how data is displayed. Differences look bigger when the y-axis doesn't start at zero. Averages can make things (like student test scores) look okay, until you realize that the data is clumped into a low and a high group.

Use Influence techniques

How to influence is covered elsewhere in this book. The challenge is deciding whether the time and effort are worth it. Choose your battles.

Meanwhile, practice influence techniques. Take the time to carefully compose comments on social media. Talk with a neutral person at work to practice sharing your opinions about how to improve a process or a function. Try calling in to a talk-radio show and share a thoughtful opinion, then be prepared to defend yourself.

As an alternative to practicing how to promote your own opinions, find people you admire who are promoting *their* opinions. You can try aligning with someone who is already an accomplished influencer. They might welcome new content to share with their followers.

The popular line, "Change comes from within" needs clarification. It is true that influence and manipulation do seem to work in this way. However, our beliefs and behaviors do not spring from within us, they are outcomes of our environment.

There is a feedback cycle of environment affecting beliefs that lead to behaviors that our environment rewards. So, deep change (such as reforming a racist) requires a stepwise process introduced into their environment that evolves their beliefs and behaviors.

This concept may seem theoretical and impractical. Think of it this way. Ads and propaganda are part of your environment. They don't implant new ideas in your mind. Instead, they connect with beliefs you already have (that come from your environment).

It should give you hope that you can make real change happen. It is easier to redesign a person's environment than directly rewire their beliefs.

Reframe problems and find common ground

Reframing is a popular technique in behavioral economics. It can help guide people to act in ways that yield better outcomes. Asking people to "opt out" rather than "opt in" can be a good thing. Your smartphone likely has strong default security settings that you can toggle off. A 401k plan may default to a recommended percentage of income (rather than zero) to be withheld for retirement savings.

You can reframe long-standing disagreements. Clarify the difference between health care reform and health care financing reform. Avoid the Pro-Choice versus Pro-Life debate by focusing on a Pro-Child policy (what do we do after birth). For people who hate working out, rather than push exercise, encourage hobbies that involve physical activity.

Finding common ground need not involve compromise. When there is disagreement in one area, search for other topics that can be agreed to. In politics, unfortunately, brinksmanship has become normal. In addition, agreement and horse-trading have been labeled falsely as compromise - and compromise to any degree is unacceptable. Find a way to show that being unyielding leads to being a loser.

Scenarios
Fringe Beliefs.
Get your friend to examine his own beliefs by listening to him and asking for clarification. Be honestly interested in what he has to say, otherwise there is no trust and he will be defensive. Encourage him to reduce his online hours per day, or partially replace some of his fringe-community time with something benign. Take your time and gradually point out gaps in data or models.

Admit that you are willing to challenge your own thinking. Share that you have researched the sources of your friend's fringe beliefs but found them lacking. Avoid being too open-minded in a way that validates his fringe beliefs. Encourage your friend to do his own research. It is not your burden to prove him wrong. You are only committing to keeping communication channels open.

Inventories.
Follow the money. Lay out the whole process associated with inventories and show how costs and time accumulate. Reframe inventory from being the net result of material-in minus material-out. Instead of being math, inventory can be seen as the result of product mix, supplier management, and marketing plans.

Homelessness.
Avoid reinventing the wheel. Find people who are already doing great work and figure out how to help. Identify experts and advocates with an unbiased view of the big picture. Help with fundraising, grants, even lawsuits.

Reframe the mental image people have of the homeless. Unsheltered addicts on the street are a visible but small part of the homeless population. Show how tackling homelessness has broad benefits for society. Affordability of housing helps everyone. Better mental health programs can enable people to be self-sufficient and reduce recurring homelessness.

Some law enforcement and court resources might be freed up as homeless rates decline.

Key points:
- Disrupt negative online and social media behaviors by pointing out how we are getting used – follow the money
- Teach people ways of thinking clearly. Try reframing a problem to shake people out of mental ruts
- Practice defending your opinions in safe situations where it is OK to fail
- Find ways to reward people who are willing to change

Start

Some inspirational quotes are paralyzing rather than inspiring. For example, "Think globally, act locally" and "Think big, start small," sound great. They seem to claim that the small stuff matters. Truth be told, they imply that you must strive for the big stuff. So, you may brain-freeze as you desperately wonder if your aspirations are worthy.

Let that go. Start small. Be excellent.

Make it personal

Start with a list of practical personal problems. Add in some passion-project challenges that matter to you. Pick a few. Ask yourself what is holding you back. If it is money, then reframe the problem in a way that you can make a difference without spending much of your own money. If you are hesitating because you don't know if you are good enough or might fail, then find someone who is making a difference and ask how you can help.

Practice communication skills. Listen to people with whom you disagree. Avoid confrontation. Seek to understand. Find the leverage points that may allow you to upend the mindsets of these people. Encourage them to think for themselves - rather than try to win an argument with them.

Meet Mr. Inflation

Wait a minute. Why is "inflation" an action item in a chapter titled "Start"? Inflation is insidious. You may not notice it from one year to the next, but it sneaks up on you. Three percent inflation over ten years reduces the purchasing power of a dollar by about 25%.

Your income, while working, needs to keep up with inflation. Your saving and investment returns need to exceed inflation. If we don't do adequate financial planning (with discipline and accepting some risk), then we'll be distracted and not useful to anyone.

Let's see the effects of inflation.

Examples of typical household inflation 1985 to 2020

Item	1985	2020	Annual Growth %
Personal computer	$4,395	$700	-5.1%
20-inch color tv	$500	$149.99	-3.4%
Bananas (1 lb)	$0.33	$0.57	1.6%
Gasoline (1 gal)	$1.12	$2.52	2.3%
Inflation average			*2.6%*
Movie ticket	$3.55	$9.16	2.7%
Honda Accord	$8,845	$24,000	2.9%
Home - median, new	$82,500	$330,800	4.0%

Item	1985	2020	Annual Growth %
Concert ticket	$15.13	$91.86	5.3%
Medicare Part B premium	$15.50	$144.60	6.6%

Source: AARP, John Waggoner, 01/24/20; *The Balance*, Dana Anspach 10/14/22

Note that inflation rates vary by sector. Technology prices can have deflation. Health care and housing have grown faster than average inflation. Anchored as we are to current prices, historical prices seem quaint, unless you are living paycheck-to-paycheck or on a fixed income. Inflation during the 1970s and after the pandemic were devastating.

Be assertive
Extract value. Spend less time on social media and news outlets. Donate to charities that provide high benefits per dollar donated. Your time and money deserve respect.

Carefully manage your performance reviews at work, so that you can speak up for yourself and ask for a raise or promotion. When your boss says no to what you want, calmly ask what it would take to perform at a higher level and be rewarded. You may find that it is time to get a new boss. Meanwhile, be honest with yourself and your family to see how to design a better work-life balance.

If you are looking for a fight

Don't shy away from aggressive actions when you feel you have been wronged. Just be clear-headed, thick-skinned and build an experienced support team of experts who believe in you.

Boycotts give a segment of consumers power. We should do something if a company's business practices are causing harm. Some harmful practices include working conditions, exploitation of labor, unfair competition, unethical foreign investments, customer discrimination, and predatory pricing. Boycotts work if consumers stay together and prove that they are in it for the long haul. Good publicity helps. The message and the desired outcome need to be simple and clear. When you see a boycott worth supporting, join and tell your friends about it.

Whistleblowing is risky. If you have access to confidential or sensitive information that proves an organization is doing something illegal or unethical, then you might pursue this path. Consult a lawyer, who should give good advice, urge caution, and take the case on contingency. Meanwhile, stay quiet and anonymous. Learn what legal protection you have. Gather only evidence that you are authorized to access and is specific to your concerns. Follow the complaint process for the proper agency and expect the process to take a long time.

Have you ever considered filing a lawsuit? You can leverage the power of the judicial system. Typical lawsuit topics include personal injury, wrongful termination at work, discrimination when buying a home, property encroachment, and replacing financial fiduciaries and trustees. Before initiating a lawsuit, consider alternatives such as negotiation, mediation, and arbitration.

Sometimes just the threat of a lawsuit can move things along. Lawsuits can be expensive, and you can't depend on lawyers working only on contingency. Talk to an attorney and make sure you have standing and a cause of action. Perhaps the best advice is to find a few people who have gone through the whole process. Buy them a cup of coffee to learn how it is done and pitfalls to avoid.

Key points:
- Don't worry about having a big impact. Start small and grow as needed
- Work on issues that matter to you
- Be assertive and thick-skinned
- Keep a steady pace and expect that success will come slowly.

Case Study: Trust

We are social creatures who belong to families, tribes, and organizations. That inter-dependence conflicts with personal values like self-reliance and freedom. If we trust the members and leaders of the groups to which we belong, then belonging is worth the lost independence.

Who does your thinking for you?
In belonging, we have roles to play. There is division of labor, and we specialize in certain skills. In particular, thinking and strategy skills are often limited to a few members of a group. For example, at work, executives do the thinking, and everyone else gets paid to do what they are told.

At home, we are busy. We act as if we don't have time to think for ourselves: About God, tax policy, what car to buy, or movies to watch. We follow media personalities. We listen to podcasts. We delegate our thinking to thought leaders and influencers.

Authority, anti-authority, and thought leaders
Choosing our thought leaders should be done carefully, as if we are betting our life-savings on a single horse race. How are we to pick a winner? Whom should we trust?

In situations where authority figures exist, we don't have a choice in thought leaders. Formal authority allows designated persons to give orders that must be followed. At times, business leaders find it helps to hire consultants to enhance their authority.

Informal authority figures gain their status based on their skills, expertise, personality, or by consensus of their followers.

Anti-authority thought leaders might have several motivations: disrupt the status quo, money, attention for themselves, a need to feel special or possess secret knowledge, or publicize a social issue. Anti-vax, for example, is not a new agenda. Vaccine methods in the 19th century were gruesome and warranted concern. Modern anti-vaccine movements are based on mistrust of government, business, and the medical profession. There is also a desire to disrupt democracy and our social order.

There are some valid reasons to mistrust authority. Sometimes politicians lie, cheat, and steal. Businesses are known to sponsor research that is biased, such as how the sugar industry demonized fat. It can be difficult to change medical best-practices when there is big money supporting the status quo, such as when a cheap cure for stomach ulcers (antibiotics and bismuth for H. pylori infections) threatened the lucrative antacid market.

Technology expands Spheres of Influence...

Prior to the printing press, literacy was limited, and documents were reproduced by hand. People looked to local representatives of royalty and religion for thought-leadership. Pronouncements, edicts, and the news were controlled by these authorities to support the status quo.

This feudal social order was disrupted by the first of three technology waves that enabled information to travel further and faster.

The post-feudal *broadcasting* wave lasted centuries. Manuscripts were replaced by printed books that could be quickly copied. Newspapers and freedom of the press could offer independent perspectives about government and public affairs. Transportation by ships, trains, and cars distributed ideas broadly. Radio and tv broadcasts made the world seem smaller. One factor remained: publishers and media networks curated the content to cover a wide range of opinions so they could attract a big audience and generate subscription and ad revenues.

The *narrowcasting* wave has lasted for decades. UHF tv stations and cable tv channels have allowed more producers of content to promote their own views. Consumers of information and entertainment have more choices. Producers must fill channels 24 hours a day with content that appeals to consumers and attracts advertisers. Channel owners can focus on their market segment, so they feel less obligated to curate content in a balanced or broad way.

The *microcasting* wave is still evolving. Internet content and social media are highly personalized and allow for extremism to scale up. Curating has been replaced by algorithms and artificial intelligence that are not accountable to oversight and can guide a consumer awry.

... and shrinks Circles of Trust

Technology powered the Renaissance and aided independent thinking. Enlightened people could extend themselves virtually, build a shared knowledge base, and innovate rapidly. Book publishers served as gatekeepers to ensure that writers met quality and accuracy standards. Scientists were subject to peer-review prior to being published.

To reach a broad audience, broadcasters had an incentive to present a range of topics and perspectives. For example, a city might have two major newspapers competing for readers. One paper might lean conservative and the other liberal, but their readers could count on broad coverage that would include most of the stories that mattered.

With narrowcasting and microcasting, consumers must be proactive to be exposed to a range of topics and opinions. That sounds a lot like work. Easier to pick a few thought leaders and passively adopt their worldviews.

Technology can generate misinformation and propaganda that are personalized and effective. The result is distrust of conflicting worldviews and their sources. Renaissance Man has become Digital Man with global reach but limited trust.

Actions that can encourage open-mindedness

Challenge bad actors. A few troublemakers can cause widespread distrust. Media companies and thought leaders can help identify these bad actors. Trying to fact-check and refute the arguments of a bad actor does not work well. They can promote ten new lies faster than one lie can be fact-checked.

Instead of countering the content, it is more effective to counter the methods bad actors use to influence followers. Put bad actors on the defensive by demanding to see their data and discrediting their experts. Force bad actors to develop a complete and coherent argument.

Foster doubt in followers. When communicating with someone who is close-minded, avoid debating their views. They will get defensive and dig in. Instead, mention that you have investigated their thought leader's views and say something like, "I tried listening to that guy, but it seems like he is always right. I just don't trust people who are never wrong." Then, say no more. Let the follower ponder, and seeds of doubt might sprout.

Reward curation. Support a certification method for thought leaders who meet standards of journalism, scientific inquiry, and political discourse. Diverse sources of information are an indicator of good thought leadership.

Demand provenance for content. To combat lies, fake news, and AI generated text or images, users should have a way to trace the source of that content. Blockchain technology is an example of creating traceability in situations that lack trust. If content sources cannot be traced, then followers should have a way to downgrade a thought leader's reputation.

Increase costs of distributing content. You probably still get junk mail delivered to your residence. It costs real money to send those letters and post cards. You get orders of magnitude more junk email than junk snail mail, because email is nearly free. Support research and regulatory methods that will make unbridled malicious content generation expensive. Perhaps, in the future, users will get paid for every search ad or junk content text they view. Barring that, there may be a way to assess an excise tax on those who generate bulk spam.

Key points:
- During the past few hundred years, technology has connected people and fostered innovation and independent thinking
- Recently, technology has enabled extremism and fringe thinking to scale up
- Even worse, technology makes us distrust opinions and information that differ from our current views
- We need to be clever at defending trust and open-mindedness

Case Study: Occupy Mars

Answer the call to action

You work for a big marketing and communications consulting firm. Which means that you influence people's opinions for a living. You got a call this afternoon that you have been reassigned to run a project team for an important client who is heavily invested in space exploration.

Congratulations. Maybe. You know next to nothing about the client or space exploration. (You may want to update your resume.)

The client has been with your firm for nearly ten years. They depend on government contracts for their revenues. Your firm's ability to influence public sentiment and garner support from members of Congress is critical. Your firm's project team has struggled. Public support for space exploration is tepid. Government funding is evaporating. Your client is threatening to jump to a competitor.

You need to turn this project around, quickly. You scheduled an all-hands team meeting for tomorrow morning. Meanwhile, you decide to do some internet research and use the Opinion-Framework to organize your thoughts.

Research to create placeholder opinions for yourself
Before the team meeting tomorrow, you gather information to answer some basic questions to understand the challenges you face.

Why go to space? (VALUES)
- Inspiration: humans need to explore, discover evidence of extraterrestrial life, learn secrets of the universe
- Survival: orbiting habitats along with colonies on the Moon or Mars can mitigate some existential threats to our species (asteroid impact, pandemic, nuclear war); space may become a platform for nation-state aggression
- Technology Transfer: tech via space exploration usually finds applications on earth. Examples so far have included robotics, advanced cameras, water purification, air filtration, solar PV, batteries, medical R&D

How much does space exploration cost? (DATA)
Initiatives are on a par with major military programs. The space station cost about $150 billion. A crewed Mars mission might be half a trillion dollars. Cost estimates likely will go up substantially.

Robotic missions work fine, why send astronauts? (MODELS)
It makes sense to have a mix of crewed and uncrewed missions. Humans can make better real-time decisions and interpret physical surroundings. On a planet or moon, they can travel better than remote rovers.

Case Study: Occupy Mars

What are the challenges for space exploration? (DATA)

Hollywood movies idealize life in space and are a disservice for managing public sentiment. In reality, space travel is cramped, smelly, unhealthy, mind-numbing, and risky. It requires precise trajectories, fuel management, and material resources. Humans require life support systems that will last reliably for years: water, food, health care, psychological wellness, radiation safety, and countering the physical effects of microgravity.

What are the key technical efforts? (MODELS)

Currently, companies are trying to lower the cost of space travel by reusing expensive components (boosters and capsules). Next, they want to put orbiting habitats above earth, the Moon, and Mars so that a mission can be done in stages. Long term, there is a vision to use materials and resources that are available in space (on the Moon or Mars or asteroids).

What are the key commercial and stakeholder issues? (VALUES)

Today's proponents of space exploration face the same problem as Kennedy did when he spoke to Congress to justify going to the moon in 1962. Most people don't care about going to space, and they think that there are better things to do with the money.

Space programs last for decades, so funding support needs to be steady regardless of which political party is in power. A business model for the space industry will need to be proven, such as tourism, low-gravity manufacturing, or rare-resource harvesting. One more thing: the public and Congress will need to come to terms with death becoming routine in space.

Always have a point of view

No matter how little you know about a problem, it helps to have an initial mental framework and a hypothesis. Sometimes, you must make decisions amidst uncertainty. The trick is to be flexible and adjust your opinion as you learn more. In this case, based on your cursory research, you might start to focus on values as the key to the project team's struggles.

For everyday people, inspiring visions about space and the future of mankind are uplifting, but that feeling doesn't last for decades. Existential threats like an asteroid impact make people feel helpless and remind them of Noah's Ark. Recall that only Noah's kin survived the flood.

You might start with the idea that a technology transfer roadmap should be the linchpin for your team's space exploration influence plan. Prove that space exploration will provide tangible benefits for people on earth (beyond Tang and cool images of hurricanes) that would not happen without space research.

The idea is to roll out new technology transfer benefits year after year, much like smartphone and car manufacturers release new features.

Your client's marketing plan would have two parts: progress reports on space exploration milestones that will take decades to achieve, and tech transfer successes that will improve life here and now. Imagine how relevant space exploration becomes if the connection is made in people's minds that every space-related challenge we overcome has an earthbound counterpart.

Life support systems that work in space should also work in extreme conditions on earth (underground, underwater, in the arctic). Advances in ways to help a half dozen people travel together in a capsule for a couple of years without killing each other should help us on earth.

Going to Mars is the stretch goal that would have the biggest impact on everyday life here on earth. Your current opinion-statement could be: We must go to Mars not because it is there and we are here, but because, on our way there, we will make life better, here.

Run the meeting and rally the team

You are as ready as you are going to be for tomorrow. The project team's morale will be low. They don't know you. Their previous leader was suddenly replaced. They have been working hard, and they will feel defensive. But what they have been doing is not working and something needs to change.

You have told them to expect an open discussion. Your tone will be to honor their past work, be realistic about their present situation, and be optimistic about the future of the project and the client relationship.

As you walk into the meeting tomorrow, your notes from this afternoon will help you guide the discussion. As you listen to your new team, be willing to toss all your notes into the wastebin. You will learn more about the root causes of the client's unhappiness and the team's struggles. Nonetheless, the basic design principle for the team's work should remain consistent: how to foster public support and secure space-exploration funding that will last for decades.

Key points:
- When faced with an opportunity where you know nothing, do some *data* research with an open mind
- Think for yourself to build your own *mental models* about the problem you face. Don't blindly accept conventional wisdom or organizational constraints
- Appeal to people's *values* as you build morale and support for a positive vision

METAPHOR OF THE SPIRIT

ORACLE OF GOD INTERNATIONAL MINISTRIES

An International Full Gospel and Deliverance Prayer Ministry

Someone once said, "They that walk; walk with the multitude. They that run! Run with a few and they that fly, fly alone". And then somebody added, "If you want to be among the many, all you need is common sense; you don't have to think before you walk. If you're going to run with the few, you need advice, but you need instruction if you're going to fly. That is why those who teach pilots to fly are called flight instructors.

Are you ready to fly? Then be instructed!

Apostle Stevie Okauru, the Oracle of God.

Founder & Senior Pastor

ORACLE OF GOD INTERNATIONAL MINISTRIES INC.

www.oraclemiracle.org/

Table Of CONTENTS

- **1** — PRAYER OF PRAISE
- **7** — THANKSGIVING PRAYER
- **25** — SUPPLICATION PRAYER
- **34** — DEFINITION OF TERM
- **45** — THE MIST METAPHOR
- **68** — THE RAIN METAPHOR
- **86** — THE RIVER METAPHOR
- **97** — THE WELL METAPHOR
- **123** — OPERATIONS OF THE SPIRIT
- **131** — ENCOUNTER WITH THE SPIRIT OF FAITH
- **151** — THE SPIRIT OF WISDOM
- **163** — HOLY SPIRIT ENCOUNTER.

CHAPTER ONE

PRAYER OF PRAISE

[Psalm 107:15-16] *"O, that men would praise the Lord for his goodness, and his wonderful works to the children of men! For He hath broken the gates of brass and cut the bars of iron in sunder."*

THE BEST PRAISERS

No matter how rich you are, it is useless in prison. No matter how strong and famous you are, it is useless if you are in jail. Adam was a powerful man. He alone was put in a garden the size of New York State. He was a very wise man. He singlehandedly named all the animals in the Garden of Eden, but he became pathetic when imprisoned. Satan physically and spiritually imprisons many, but the Almighty God has broken the gates of brass and cut the bars of iron in sunder. That is why we can now say we are Free. Can you praise God heartily for that? And as you praise Him, may He lift you mightily in the Name of Jesus Christ. Amen!

Prayer is powerful! We communicate with God in prayer and get the result when we do so according to His will. But when we praise Him, we acknowledge His personality? When we give Him thanks, we celebrate Him for what He has done, for what He is doing, and for what He will do. And then, in worship, we appreciate the Lord for who He is. And Jehovah expects all creation to worship Him in spirit and truth. **[John 4:24]**

CATEGORIES OF PRAISERS

Nevertheless, there are various categories of worshippers. One category of worshippers is those who, at one time or the other, received a blessing from God and worshiped Him for that but **[Psalm 150:6]** *"Let everything that has breath praise the Lord!"*

No matter how little we think the goodness of God in our life may be, we must praise Him, for He created us to praise Him. We are a creation of praise. **[Isaiah 43:7]** *"Everyone who is called by My name, whom I have created for My glory...."*

The second category of worshippers is the afflicted praisers. These include the bereaved, the sorrowful, the disappointed, and the discouraged. A classic example is Mr. Job. He worshipped God in prosperity **[Job 1:1-4],** he continued to worship Him amid afflictions **[Job**

1:15 to Job 2:10] until his turnaround breakthrough came **[Job 42:12-16]**.

The third category of worshippers is the vessels unto dishonor **[1st Timothy 2:20-21]. The devil uses them** to change joy to sorrow. They are satanic agents.

And there is yet a fourth category of worshippers; the vessels unto honor **[1st Timothy 2:20-21]**. A vessel unto honor is someone God can use anytime, anyway, and anywhere He wants to. And in whatever condition to show forth His glory. They are chosen and empowered by God. **[John 15:16]**.

Such people are willing to be used and ready to live a holy lifestyle.

Are you a vessel unto honor? If yes, always give the Lord high praises. If you are not a vessel of honor, I urge you to repent and cry unto God for mercy now.

May the Lord make and keep you a vessel unto honor in Jesus' Name. Amen!

I pray that the Lord will give you a grateful heart and the grace to praise Him always in Jesus' Name. Amen!

MAGNIFY THE LORD

Magnify His Holy Name! He is worthy of being praised and adored! He has released us from physical and spiritual prison! Our breakthrough has come! Our glory will now shine forth!

So, lift Him high! He is our Maker! So, worship Him! Worship the God of breakthroughs.

Lord! You are highly exalted; there is no one like You. You are the Highest! Eternal Rock of Ages, King of Kings! Lord of Lords! The I AM that I AM, the Lion of the Tribe of Judah! Glory be to Your Holy! Thank You for the breakthrough! Thank You for life!

Thank You for joy! Thank You for salvation! Thank You for healing and deliverance! Accept our worship in Jesus' Name. Amen!

PRAISE QUOTE

"The more you praise and celebrate your life, the more there is in life to celebrate." – **OPRAH WINFREY.**

CHAPTER TWO

THANKSGIVING PRAYER

[Psalm 92:1] *"It is a good thing to give thanks to the Lord and to sing praises unto His Holy Name ..."*

THE POWER OF THANKSGIVING

Ignorance is no excuse in law. And when the law of life is broken like most laws, whether spiritual, physical, medical, etc., we become victims. **[Hosea 4:6]** says, *"My people are destroyed for lack of knowledge."* We are His people, yet we are suffering from a lack of knowledge;

we need to know to be free because we do not know the truth.

Many are grounded because they take God for granted. When we take God for granted, we get grounded sooner or later. A simple thank you is what qualifies us for the next act of favor from our benefactors. Many have had great times in the past, but the great times have turned into gloomy days because they did not acknowledge and appreciate the source of those great times. So, the one behind the great times withdrew and turned his back at them.

It is a worthy addition to be addicted to giving God thanks. Just as alcoholics are addicted to wine and smokers to cigarettes, you too can become an addict to thanksgiving. When you become addicted to thanksgiving, destiny opens to you on its own accord. **[Psalm 92:1].**

Good things begin to come to us when we thank God, which is a good thing, and no one can hurt us! **[1st Peter 3:13].**

Thanksgiving envelopes us in God; we become untouchable and unshakeable. We become inaccessible by demons, warlocks, witches, and fetish because we are enveloped in divine presence. Divine presence covers you when you are a person of thanksgiving.

God doesn't need our money; He wants our appreciation. He doesn't need our stuff; He wants to stuff us with all kinds of good stuff. The only thing God cannot give to Himself is praise and thanksgiving! That is why God is always with those who always praise Him and give Him thanks. **[Psalm 22:3]**.

And nothing is more valuable than divine presence in our lives in the race of life. **[Psalm 16:11]** says, *"In His presence is fullness of joy and pleasures always."* Thanksgiving is not about things that happen to us, and we feel we should give thanks because it is the "right thing" to do. Thanksgiving qualifies us for God's divine presence when done with spiritual understanding and sincerely from the heart. And God's presence is all we need to have a most triumphant ride in life. Moses said in **[Exodus 33:15]**, *"If thy presence goes not with me, carry us not up hence."*

[Romans 8:31] says, *"... If God is for us, who can be against us?* God won't be with us because we cry; he will be with us only because we praise Him. So, when we give in to praise and thanksgiving, we qualify for the divine presence. And when we carry divine presence, it makes all the difference. When God goes with you, everything goes great for you! **[Psalm 16:11]**.

Prayer is good; fasting is great; giving is wonderful, but none of these qualifies us for God's divine presence. Our prayers give God an extra job. Our giving is to bring the blessings of God in our lives and to turn God's favor in our direction. There is nothing God is benefiting from us, except the "thank you Lord" and "the bless your Holy Name." It is out of what He has given us that we give back to God. What you don't have, you can't give.

When you praise Him, you attract Him! And when you attract Him, everything goes attractive for you. And our degree of gratitude defines the greatness of our journey in life. Gratitude is what determines our ultimate altitude in life. The more grateful we are, the more colorful and glorious our destiny becomes. It is a worthy addition to be grateful to God.

We are stranded in life because we are addicted to complaints and murmurings. And **[1st Corinthians 10:10 TLB]** *"And don't murmur against God and his dealings with you as some of them did, for that is why God sent his Angel to destroy them."*

Complaints may look logical, but they will only make your situation even more critical. Complaints may sound logical, but thanksgiving is the only Biblical way forward and upward. It is the only lawful way forward in your pursuit. When we are committed to thanksgiving, we attract unsolicited favor.

Many pray fervently, but they don't give thanks fervently. And thanksgiving is far more potent than prayers. When you pray, God answers you if He hears; it is not all prayers that He hears; He said if we pray according to His will, He hears. But when you give thanks and praise Him, He comes down.

And when God comes down, your Pharaoh must bow out; when God came down to Egypt, Pharaoh bow into the red sea. When you praise God, He comes down to see to the operation by Himself. And if God is for you, who can be against you! That is how powerful thanksgiving is in the race of life. When you praise God, He comes down and envelopes you; He puts you inside Himself so that the arrows of the wicked can't touch you.

And prayer has technicalities; you must pray according to the will of God; to receive an answer; so, you can pray amiss. But interestingly, you can't praise God amiss. You praise Him anyhow; He takes it in any language, He takes it in any art form. You don't need to quote any scripture to praise God acceptably; praise Him from the depth of your heart. He said, is anyone happy with me and what I am doing? Let him sing. That makes thanksgiving an open check for every believer. You can praise your way into fortune, glory, and beauty. David praised his way into the heart of God. The Bible calls him a man after God's own heart. In **[Psalm 119:164]**, David gives thanks and praise seven times a day. And prays only three times a day. And you can see how many marks he made on earth.

In 1996 Israel celebrated David's 3000 years of naming Jerusalem the city of David. He was so lost in God that his name became as eternal as God. You can praise your way into the heart of God. If you must be remembered after your tenure on earth; you must get lost in God. And to get lost in God is to give Him thanks and praise Him. Thank Him for what He is done. Praise Him for who He is. If God still means anything to you, praise is the only way to show it. If you live with that attitude of gratitude, destiny opens to you in a grand style.

POWER OF GIVING THANKS

There is nothing more potent than the force of thanksgiving. In **[Matthew 14:13-21]**, Jesus fed five thousand men with five loaves of bread and two fishes, and women and children were not counted. He took the five loaves of bread, and two fishes lifted His hands and gave thanks to God and miracles erupted. Thanksgiving is a very fertile platform for the eruption of miracles, signs, and wonders. Nothing goes down with a thanks giver. Everything rises in the hands of a thanks giver. Thanksgiving is the catalyst that boosts every destiny. ***We begin to*** *move and expand to unimaginable new heights as we praise and thank God!*

THANKSGIVING DO THE IMPOSSIBLE

Also, in **[John 11]**, Jesus got to the tomb of Lazarus, dead and buried after four days, and Jesus lifted His hands and said, Father, I thank you! As He gave thanks, death was converted to life. *No matter what has died in your life, when you give thanks from the depth of your heart, they come back to life in Jesus' Name. Amen!*

Thanksgiving is not just a pause in prayers. It is not what you do because you are told you must do it; it is what you know and why you are doing it. When you know why you are doing it, you begin to tap into the blessings of thanksgiving. Nothing grows in your hands without thanksgiving. **[Psalm 67:5-6]** *"Let the* *peoples praise You, O God; let all the peoples praise You. Then the earth shall yield her increase; God, our own God, shall bless us."* **Nothing rises or increases in your life without thanksgiving and praise.**

ATTITUDE OF GRATITUDE BRINGS FAVOR

Praising and returning thanks to God makes all the difference. If you cannot see anything He has done, you are not ready for the next thing you desire. Until you can see what He has done, you are not qualified to see the next things you desire done. God does things every day; you sleep and wake up; because God sustained you, so thank Him. It is not the alarm that woke you. The alarm cannot bring to life. And your life is your greatest asset? Nothing compares in value with your life. So, the one sustaining that life is worthy of your thanks and praise. **[Psalm 150:6]** says, *"Let everything that has breath praise the Lord."* Not everything that has a car, a job, house, spouse, etc. Let everything that has breathed praise God. You are not alive by chance; the one who kept you on your feet is worthy of appreciation. He is worthy of honor and adoration.

And many are alive but crying because they have no shoes and clothes. Somebody has shoes and clothes but has no life. We are so bothered and burdened about minor things: That is why thanksgiving becomes an uphill task. Whatever force that kept you on your feet till today requires your attention in thanksgiving and praise. And I am sure you know it is not the devil that kept you alive; it is God. Satan doesn't keep anybody alive; he is the thief; *he comes to kill, steal, and destroy.* **[John10:10]**. So, if you are alive; it is God that put you on your feet; Jesus made it possible. So, respond with thanksgiving.

Until you truly resign yourself to God, your journey will always be tough and rough. You owe God thanks; it is a debt you must pay and pay now and forever! The thanksgiving we hold in the church is to stimulate our thanksgiving attitude to God.

DELIVERANCE POWER OF THANKS AND PRAISE

In **[Acts 16:16-26]**, Paul and Silas were awaiting execution; in **verse 25,** at midnight, as they switched to praise, God came down in an earthquake and delivered them. Thanksgiving and praise are weapons of deliverance.

When an evil spirit came upon King Saul, David sang, and the evil spirit departed from King Saul. When you are sold out to a life of thanksgiving and praise, evil spirits can't hold you to ransom. God, by His divine presence, delivers you.

Paul and Silas prayed and sang praise to God; the other prisoners mocked them, but God freed them. People may mock you; as you praise Him, they may say we can't even see why he is still praising God. *But as they mock you, God will step in to free you. As you praise Him, you shall not remain in chains anymore in Jesus' Name. Amen!*

Ingratitude finishes good things in our lives. When we switch to gratitude, we will never again experience emptiness! Nothing goes empty when your thanksgiving to God is full. Thanksgiving terminates emptiness. The food on our table today, God put it there. He gave us the job we have today. Smarter and more qualified people are jobless. The strength to work the job God gave to us. So, everything about our life is a gift from God. **What role did you play to be born?** Thanksgiving and praise are the cheapest way to recognize that God is why you and I are alive today. He is the reason for the seasons we see. the reason for the blessings that we enjoy. God is the reason for the breath in our nostrils and the food we eat. God is the reason for the peace in our family. The reason for everything that people applaud us for. He is the reason for all the goodness in our lives. So, God is worthy of all our thanks, and praise. So, let's thank the Almighty God now.

APPRECIATE THE LORD

Father, we want to bless Your Name. Thank You for being so good! For being so kind! For being so wonderful! Thank You for loving us! For saving our soul! Thank You for what You did for us in the past! Thank You for a new beginning! Glory be to Your Holy Name, Lord! Thank You for keeping us alive, that You for eyes to see, ears to hear, a mouth that can still shout, hands that can still clap, legs that can still dance. Thank You, Lord, for all the blessings in Jesus' Precious Name. Amen!

THANKSGIVING QUOTE

"Gratitude opens the door, the power, the wisdom, the creativity of the universe. You open the door through gratitude." - **Deepak Chopra**

CHAPTER THREE

--- ★ ---

SUPPLICATION PRAYER

[Ephesians 6:18] *'Praying at all times in the Spirit, with all prayer and supplication. To that end, keep alert with all perseverance, making supplication for all the saints."*

WHAT IS PRAYER OF SUPPLICATION?

We come to God in prayer for a variety of reasons. To worship Him, confess our sins, and ask for forgiveness. We thank Him for His blessings, we ask for things for ourselves, and we pray for the needs of others.

The Hebrew and Greek words most often translated "supplication" in the Bible means *"a request or petition."* So, a prayer of supplication is asking God for something. Unlike the prayer of petition, which is praying on behalf of others, supplication is generally a request for the person praying.

The Bible includes many prayers of supplication, especially in the Psalms. David's Psalms are filled with supplication for mercy in **[Psalm 4:1]**, for divine direction and divine leading in **[Psalm 5:8]**, for deliverance in [Psalm 6:4], for salvation from persecution in **[Psalm 7:1]**, and so on.

When Daniel learned that King Darius had issued an edict prohibiting prayer to any god but the king, Daniel continued to pray to God with prayers of thanksgiving as well as prayers of supplication for His help in that dire situation.

In the New Testament, Jesus admonishes us to ask for our daily bread in **[Matthew 6:11]**, which falls into the category of a prayer of supplication. In **[Luke 18:1-8]**, Jesus teaches us not to give up praying for what we need. James said: we don't receive because we don't ask **[James 4:2]**. And when we do ask, we don't receive; because we are thinking only of our fleshly desires **[James 4:3]**. So, the best way to approach God in supplication is to ask, in all honesty, modesty, as children talking to their kind-hearted Father but ending with *"Lord Let Your will be done."* **[Matthew 26:39]**.

[Ephesians 6:13-18] *"Therefore take up the whole armor of God, that you may be able to withstand in the evil day, and having done all, to stand. Stand therefore, having girded your waist with truth, having put on the breastplate of righteousness, and having shod your feet with the* *preparation of the gospel of peace; above all, taking the shield of faith with which, you will be able to quench all the fiery darts of the wicked one. And take the helmet of salvation, and the sword of the Spirit, which is the word of God; always praying with all prayer and supplication in the Spirit, being watchful to this end with all perseverance and supplication for all the saints."* In this passage, after describing the need to take up the **"full armor of God,"**

Apostle Paul exhorted the Ephesians [and us] to remain always alert and to pray in the Spirit, *"Making supplication for all the saints."* **[Ephesians 6:18]**. Prayers of supplication are part of the spiritual battle all believers engage in; we relieve anxieties by faithful prayers, especially prayers of thanksgiving and supplication.

This is the formula for ensuring that "the peace of God, which surpasses all understanding, will guard our hearts and minds in Christ Jesus. **[Philippians 4:6-7]** *"Be anxious for nothing, but in everything by prayer and supplication, with thanksgiving, let your requests be made known to God; ⁷ and the peace of God, which surpasses all understanding, will guard your hearts and minds through Christ Jesus."*

In **[Philippians 4:6-7],** we see another crucial aspect of the prayer of supplication: we see the necessity of faith in the Lord Jesus Christ. Those who belong to Christ also have the indwelling Holy Spirit who intercedes on their behalf. Because we often don't know what or how to pray as we ought to when we approach God. The Holy Spirit intercedes and prays for us, interpreting our supplications so that, when we are overwhelmed by trials and the cares of life, He lends assistance with our prayers of supplication, sustaining us before the throne of grace. **[Romans 8:26]** *'Likewise the Spirit also helps in our weaknesses. For we do not know what we should pray for as we ought, but the Spirit Himself makes intercession for us with groanings which cannot be uttered."*

PRAYER OF SUPPLICATION AND PETITION

PRAYER 1: *Eternal Rock of Ages, I ask in the Name of Your Son Jesus Christ to please bless, heal, restore, and promote my loved ones by the power in the Blood of Jesus and me.*

PRAYER 2: *Father Lord, please let all my requests be granted, and let my mouth be filled with laughter. For in the name of Jesus Christ, I pray.*

PRAYER 3: *Holy Spirit, I don't want to remain where I was last year. Lord,* *take me to the next level! Father, I don't want to remain where I was last year, physically, materially, spiritually, take me to the next level!*

PRAYER 4: *El-Shaddai, I don't want to be stagnant anymore. From now on, let my progress be rapid in Jesus' Mighty Name. Amen!*

PRAYER 5: *Holy Father, anything or anyone that will not allow me to serve you more this year, remove them, O Lord!*

PRAYER 6: *Lord Jesus, I know this will be a special year; don' let me miss my time of visitation! Go ahead, talk to the Almighty! Don't let me miss my own time of visitation.*

PRAYER 7: The Bible says that you shall decree a thing and be established unto you. *Father, I* *decree, every wall of Jericho in my path, to fall flat tonight!*

PRAYER 8: *Thank God for answering your prayers.*

SUPPLICATION QUOTE

"Relationships can't blossom unless there is meaningful communication. That's why 'supplication is the key to worship.' It is a sign of meaningful communication between God and a person." - **Suhaib Webb**

CHAPTER FOUR

DEFINITION OF TERM

[John 3:7-9] *"Do not marvel that I said to you, 'You must be born again.' The wind blows where it wishes, and you hear it but cannot tell where it comes from and where it goes. So is everyone who is born of the Spirit." Nicodemus answered and said to Him, "How can these things be?"*

WHAT IS METAPHOR?

A metaphor is a figure of speech in which a word or phrase is applied to an object or action to which it is not applicable. A metaphor is regarded as representative or symbolic of something else, especially something abstract. Some synonyms of metaphor include a *figure of speech, figurative expression, image, trope, allegory, parable and adages, analogy, symbol · emblem, story, tale, myth, legend, saga, fable, and apologue. Etc.*

DEFINING SPIRIT

One online Bible dictionary definition of 'spirit' is the non-physical part of a person's seat of emotions and character: the soul. Our spirit is the non-physical part of our true self that can survive physical death or separation from the body. The Bible says in **[1ˢᵗ Thessalonians 5:23 KJ21]** *"And the very God of peace sanctify you wholly, and I pray God your whole spirit and soul and body be preserved* *blameless unto the coming of our Lord Jesus Christ."*

So, man is spirit; he has a soul and lives inside a body. God also is Spirit **[John 4:24]** *"God is Spirit, and those who worship Him must worship in spirit and truth."*

METAPHOR OF THE SPIRIT

Here is what God is doing globally in terms of the move of the Holy Spirit, which I will put in a framework termed **'the metaphor of the Spirit about water.'** There are many symbols or representations of the Holy Spirit in the Scripture, like **Dove, Fire, Wind, Water, etc. Let's deal with the metaphor of the Spirit about Water.**

HOMILETIC OF SCRIPTURE

[John 7:37-39] *"On the last day, that great day of the feast, Jesus stood* *and cried out, saying, "If anyone thirsts, let him come to Me and drink. He who believes in me, as the Scripture has said, out of his heart shall Flow Rivers of living water."* **[AND HE GAVE THE MEANING OF THE METAPHOR IN VERSE 39]** *But this He spoke concerning the Spirit, whom those believing in Him would receive; for the Holy Spirit was not yet given because Jesus was not yet glorified."*

So, The Word is saying Rivers will flow out of you. The significant thing about rivers flowing out of an individual is a type of metaphor of the Holy Spirit or a manifestation of the Holy Spirit.

HOMILETIC PRINCIPLES

Homiletics is the study of the human aspect. Homiletics involves the study of **everything related to the art of preparing and preaching sermons**. Good sermons [communication] are birthed out of good communion [companionship] and fellowship. Proficiency in the art of scriptural homiletic is vital because adequate preaching and teaching ministry are essential to growth and spiritual development. Any lack or ministerial deficiency in this area will impoverish congregations and stifle the spiritual growth of individual members of the church.

Therefore, learning the art of sermon preparation and delivery becomes a crucial part of the life of every minister of God. Nevertheless, when we interpret the scripture, there are requirements and guidelines for us to understand various positions of the Scripture. And most times, *in the study of "Scriptural Homiletics,"* you must interpret the scriptures as literally as possible. But that is often not possible because such literal interpretations would not make sense. Because some metaphors of the Scriptures are so deep that if you interpret them literally, it will produce a great error. For example, when the Bible, in **[Psalm 91:4]**, says, *"He shall cover you with His feathers, and under His wings, you shall take refuge; His truth shall be your shield and buckler."*

This doesn't mean that God is a big bird! But we understand that it is a metaphor.

Another example is **[Jeremiah 1:11-12]** *"Moreover the Word of the LORD came to me, saying, "Jeremiah, what do you see?" And I said, "I see a branch of an almond tree." Then the LORD said to me, "You have seen well, for I am ready to perform My Word."*

The Lord tells Prophet Jeremiah that it is my Word even though you see an almond tree! This also is a metaphor for scripture. And this, too, is true when we are dealing with things like water in the scripture.

METAPHORIC FORMS OF WATER IN SCRIPTURE

There are seven forms of waters in the Scriptures.

1. **MIST**
2. **DEW**
3. **RAIN**
4. **RIVERS**
5. **WELLS**
6. **SEAS**
7. **THE WATERS ABOVE AND THE WATERS BENEATH.**

These seven distinct metaphoric forms of water in the scriptures are very significant because they deal with seven distinct manifestations of the Holy Spirit. And we experience these from time to time in our Christian walk.

THE DEMONIC METAPHOR OF WATER IN SCRIPTURE

Whenever you have water mentioned in the scripture, it is either a manifestation of the Holy Spirit or a manifestation of a rising of a demonic system. **[Isaiah 59:19]** says, *"So shall they fear the name of the Lord from the west, and his glory from the rising of the sun. When the enemy shall come in like a flood, the Spirit of the Lord shall lift a standard against him."*

Also, in **[Revelation 12:15-16]**, *"And the serpent cast out of his mouth water as a flood after the woman, that he might cause her to be carried away of the flood. And the earth helped the woman, and the earth opened her mouth, and swallowed up* *the flood which the dragon cast out of his mouth."*

Another instant was in **[Matthew 14:22-33]** when Jesus walked on water. The wind was blowing water into the boat. And Peter said to Jesus, if it is you let me walk on water to you. That manifestation was not to edify and build the Church. It was a destructive demonic system.

- So, when Peter asked to walk on water, he was permitted to walk on a demonic system.

- He was given authority over a demonic system.

- And when the water was entering the boat, it was the demonic system attempting to infiltrate the church and sink or drown it.

- The twelve Apostles were bailing out water, keeping the system of Babylon out of the boat [or out of the Church of God].

So, we must understand that; there is also this interpretation of water in the scripture.

SPIRIT QUOTE

"A free spirit takes liberties even with liberty itself. "– **Francis Picabia**

[2nd Corinthians 3:17] King James Version

"Now the Lord is that Spirit: and where the Spirit of the Lord is, there is liberty."

CHAPTER FIVE

---·★·---

THE MIST METAPHOR

[2nd Peter 2:17] *"These are springs without water and mists driven by a storm, for whom the black darkness has been reserved."*

Mist is caused by particles of water vapor filling the air until it is only partially transparent. Mist and haze produce much the same effect, the one being due to moisture in the atmosphere and the other to dust particles. Mist or fog is not common on the plains of Palestine and Syria at sea level, but it is of almost daily occurrence in the mountain valleys, coming up at night and disappearing with the morning sun.

In the account of creation, **"there went up a mist from the earth,"** giving a description of the warm, humid atmosphere of the carboniferous ages which agrees remarkably with modern science **[Genesis 2:6]** *"But a mist went up from the earth and watered the whole face of the ground."*

The word mist is used figuratively or metaphorically in **[Acts 13:11]** to describe the shutting out of light. **[Acts 13:11]** *"And now, indeed, the hand of the Lord is upon you, and you shall be blind, not seeing the sun for a time." And immediately a dark* **mist fell on him,** *and he went around seeking someone to lead him by the hand."*

Those who bring confusion and uncertainty are compared metaphorically in scripture to *"mists driven by a storm"* [2nd **Peter 2:17**]. *"These are wells without water, clouds carried by a tempest, for whom is reserved the blackness of darkness forever."*

The mist was first mentioned in the Bible in **[Genesis 2]**; then, the whole earth was watered by mist. The entire earth was one mass land. **[Genesis 10:25]** says, **"The earth was divided in the days of Peleg. So, the earth in Adam's days was one huge landmass."**

And the reason mist, not rain, was sent all through the earth was because there was no human activity yet on the earth. **[Genesis 2:5]**

THE MIST METAPHOR

[Genesis 2:6] *"But a mist went up from the earth and watered the whole face of the ground."*

The mist was just enough provision for managing a world view or a world vision. If you don't have the mist of the Holy Spirit in your life, you will never have a global vision of your endeavors, of your talent, and your gifts. If you don't have mist, you can't have a global perspective of your local commission, mission, ministry, church, business, etc. But if you begin to think globally from your present vicinity and positioning, it will trigger the Holy Ghost mist upon your life and your endeavor to a global dimension.

Mist moistens the ground; it cannot cause an overflow. But it is essential to have mist to moisten the ground. And that causes the ecosystem of life to stay vibrated and alive. And the reason we don't have ecological systems in many ministries, destinies, and families, which is a portion of the Holy Spirit; that is supposed to keep the ministry or destiny alive, is because there is no global vision. ***We all need a global vision!***

We must have a global vision; we must look beyond the four walls of our ministries. Everyone has an inert, irrevocable value; you have something in you that can touch the world globally. Whether it is, it may be the ability to make a cake, sew a dress, teach, preach a sermon, write a book, or create revenue on all kinds of levels. Every one of us has a global touch. We can touch the world. And many times, we never reach that goal because the mist of the Holy Ghost never blows into our lives. We are not moisturized by the Holy Spirit's mist, which is essential for the next level. ***Say Holy Spirit! Moisturize my life for the next level!***

MIST QUOTE

"Mist to mist drops to drops. For water thou art, and unto water shalt thou return." — **Kamand Kojouri**

THE DEW METAPHOR

[Genesis 27:28] *"Therefore, God give thee of the dew of heaven, and the fatness of the earth, and plenty of corn and wine:"*

The second metaphor of the spirit about water is dew. Dew in **[Genesis]** only falls in the garden. The Bible says the Garden of Eden was watered by dew. Not the whole earth, but only the Garden. Dew as a manifestation of the Spirit comes because of what you do. To enhance what you do locally for increase globally. It's your own Garden, your ministry, your job, your career, your business, and your handiwork. The Bible says God will bless the works of your hand. *"The Lord will open to you His good treasure, the heavens, to give the rain to your land in its season, and to bless all the work of your hand."* **[Deuteronomy 28:12].**

So, no occupation, no dew, no Garden, no dew. The smaller your Garden; the small the dew you receive; the bigger the Garden, the bigger the dew you receive.

Adam's Garden was about three thousand square miles long. So, in the confines of his Garden, he was getting moisture more than the rest of the earth. The rest of the earth was getting mist, but Adam's Garden got more than mist; it got mist and dew, a double portion. The dew of the Holy

Spirit introduces a double portion upon your life's endeavors.

And the double portion in Adam's Garden was causing a very luscious environment. The dew was creating greater foliage because God told Adam that; in your Garden, not the rest of the earth, but your garden, I have planted every conceivable tree; that is fruit or meat for you and generations after you. And they were sustained because of the dew that dropped in his Garden. **[Genesis 2]**.

The point is, if you have a small garden, you will receive small dew; a small Garden means small trees; with small trees, you receive limited fruits. Limited fruits equal limited energy. So, The Onus is on us as individuals to expand our tent, lengthen our cords, enlarge our coast, develop our Gardens, ministries, businesses on a much broader scale. **[Isaiah 54:2]** says, *"Enlarge the place of your tent and let them stretch out the curtains of your dwellings; Do not spare; lengthen your cords and strengthen your stakes."*

Suppose you don't broaden your imagination and move by faith. In that case, you can't get enough dews to release the promises of the Word and the Holy Spirit that you are confessing, prophesying, decreeing, and declaring. If you don't do that, you will not have enough foliage for a prosperous life. And you need this foliage so that you can have massive covering for your region. **[Galatians 6:9 NIV]** says, *"Let us not become weary in doing good, for at the proper time we will reap a harvest if we do not give up."* If you are not weary in doing good in due [that is time] and dew in terms of moisture in due season, you shall reap.

In **[Genesis 27]**, Isaac, after blessing Jacob, Esau showed up. And he said, the father gives me at least one blessing; the only thing he was given was the dew. In other words, Esau, if you can build your own Garden, even though the major blessing did not fall on your life, one thing is guaranteed; the dew of heaven will water your garden, and one day, you will take dominion. *I prophesy! No matter how insignificant you are now, no matter what part of the earth you might find yourself; No matter how small you may start; If you can start that Garden, there is a move of the Holy Spirit that would force dew upon your life in the Name of Jesus Christ. Amen!*

Say, Lord Jesus! Force the dew of heaven upon my life in the Name of Jesus!

Gideon understood this principle; he said to God, if this is you talking to me, I don't want a flood-like Elijah, I don't want rivers to overflow, all I want is the dew to fall on my land. If the dew falls on my land and this fleece is dry, then I know that it's on, and it did. The next day, he says, if the dew falls on this fleece but not on the land, then I know that you are with me and that you got my back. **[Judges 6:37; Judges 6:38; Judges 6:39 Judges 6:40].** *God gave Gideon the blessing of dew! If God is with you, who can be against you! If God is with you, you will receive your dew of blessings in due time.*

Say Lord bring me the dew of blessing in due time!

Gideon accessed the dew level of the Holy Spirit, where God blessed the work of his hands. Dew is divine favor! ***Say Lord give me divine favor by Your Spirit in the Name of Jesus!***

You can be in the most God forsaking place on the earth; You can be in the slums of Nairobi Kenya, or Soweto South Africa; or Ajegunle in Lagos Nigeria, if you have the dew of heaven upon your life, you will begin to have the works of your hands blessed, as God sends the dew of heaven upon you.

Dew is not violent in the outpouring, but it is consistent and sustains what you are doing. It takes you from one level to the next; your ground will always be moist. When you have dew in your life, you don't have to depend on the water table because the water table fluctuates according to various dynamics. Dew means that all your days, you will work in favor. ***Say, O Lord My God, grant me divine favor!***

THE BLESSING OF DEW

The word *"dew"* appears 34 times in the Old King James Version Bible, and it is primarily seen as a blessing. It is used metaphorically, poetically, and symbolically in many places of scripture and is quite different from the blessing of rain. Since Passover, Jewish people across the land have been praying the *"Tfilat Tal"* – a prayer or blessing for dew, asking God to bring light out of the darkness to draw Israel to himself, as a root finds water from dew.

Rain will always catch our attention, as anyone caught out in the rain would know. It can be heard in raindrops' pitter-patter or the pummeling of a heavy shower. But dew, on the other hand, is silent. It does not draw attention to itself at all. It can be seen as a more humble, unassuming version of rain – never causing damage; gentle, nourishing, and dependable. ***Glory to God!***

UNIQUENESS OF DEW OF THE SPIRIT?

Dew often goes unnoticed, and we need to be aware of this subtle gift from God that speaks of his steadfast love – his mercies and favor that come anew every morning.

As with so many concepts we read about in the Bible, the first-time dew is mentioned in blessing is key in understanding the significance of its metaphor. In **[Genesis 27:28]**, Isaac blesses Jacob with these words: *"May God give you the dew of heaven and the fatness of the earth…."*

Dew speaks divine blessing metaphorically. It is seen to descend with the manna and the quail God provided for Israel in the desert. It is a refreshment, a gift, and a source of life- **[Exodus 16]**. The blessing of rain is well-known and understood. God sends rain as a blessing and withholds it when he wants to correct and draw our attention back to himself. Rain is not just a tool of blessing but can also be a curse if it is the wrong type of rain at the wrong time and season. A heavy downpour can destroy an entire crop of wheat or barley if it comes too late or too early in the season.

On the other hand, Dew shows up early every morning, unconditionally. And it is always a blessing. It sustains, bringing gentle nourishment to our spirit, soul, and body. Whether or not we pay attention to it, dew is always there, regardless. And however long we may have ignored it or been oblivious to its presence, it appears day after day; no questions asked... just like the unconditional love of God.

SOME DEW SCRIPTURES

[Genesis 27:39] "And Isaac his father answered and said unto him, Behold, thy dwelling shall be the fatness of the earth, and **the dew of heaven from above.**"

[Exodus 16:13] "And it came to pass, that at even the quails came up, and covered the camp: and **in the morning the dew lay round about the host.**"

[Numbers 11:9] "And when the **dew fell upon the camp in the night**, the manna fell upon it."

[Deuteronomy 32:2] "My doctrine shall drop as the rain, **my speech shall distill as the dew,** as the small rain upon the tender herb, and as the showers upon the grass:"

[Deuteronomy 33:13] "And of Joseph he said, Blessed of the LORD be his land, for the precious things of heaven, **for the dew,** and the deep that couches beneath."

[Job 29:19] "My root was spread out by the waters, and **the dew lay all night upon my branch.**"

[Job 29:22] "After a word from me, they did not speak again; **my speech settled on them like dew.**"

[Job 38:28] "Hath the rain a father? **Or who hath begotten the drops of dew?**"

[Psalm 65:12] "**The wilderness pastures drip with dew,** and the hills wrap themselves with joy."

[Proverbs 3:20] "By his knowledge, the depths are broken up, and **the clouds drop down the dew.**"

[Proverbs 19:12] "The king's wrath is as the roaring of a lion, **but his favor is as dew upon the grass.**"

[Hoses 6:4] *"O Ephraim, what shall I do unto thee? O Judah, what shall I do unto thee? For your goodness is as a morning cloud, and as **the early dew it goeth away.**"*

[Hosea 14:5] *"**I will be as the dew unto Israel:** he shall grow as the lily and cast forth his roots as Lebanon."*

[Micah 5:7] *"And the remnant of Jacob shall be amid many people **as a dew from the LORD,** as the showers upon the grass, that tarrieth not for man, nor waiteth for the sons of men."*

[Haggai 1:10] *"**Therefore, the heaven over you stays from dew,** and the earth stays from her fruit."*

VERSES OF DEW AND THEIR METAPHOR

#1. *"Your people will offer themselves freely on the day of your* *power, in holy garments; **from the womb of the morning, the dew of your youth will be yours**.*" **[Psalm 110:3]**.

In this metaphor, the morning's womb infers the very break of the morning when dew appears. It speaks of freshness, the strength of the early stages of life. It lets us know that God, like dew, will always provide the sustenance we need.

#2. *"[unity] is like the dew of Hermon, which falls on the mountains of Zion!*

For there the Lord has commanded the blessing, life always." **[Psalm 133:3]**.

Here, the Psalmist metaphorically writes of God's great joy in our unity: **"How good and pleasant it is when brothers dwell together in unity!"** This is like dew, which is connected to God's life-giving blessing.

#3. *"I will be like the dew to Israel; he shall blossom like the lily; he shall take root like the trees of Lebanon his shoots shall spread out; his beauty shall be like the olive, and his fragrance like Lebanon."* **[Hosea 14:5-6]**.

In this verse, God metaphorically likens Himself to Dew, a great blessing to us that causes flourishing, growth, beauty, and fragrance.

'THE HEBREW BLESSING FOR DEW.'

May dew fall upon the blessed land. Fill us with heaven's finest blessings. May light come out of the darkness to draw Israel to you as a root finds water from dew. May you bless our food with dew.

May we enjoy plenty with nothing lacking—Grant the wish of the people

– that followed you through the desert-like sheep – with dew.

You are Adonai our God, who causes the wind to blow and the dew to fall, For blessing and not curse. Amen. For life and not for death. Amen. For plenty and not for lack. Amen.

What a wonderful prayer!

DEW QUOTE

"In the sweetness of friendship, let there be laughter and sharing of pleasures. For in the dew of little things, the heart finds its morning and is refreshed." - **Khalil Gibran.**

CHAPTER SIX

THE RAIN METAPHOR

[Leviticus 26:4] *"Then I will give you rain in due season, and the land shall yield her increase, and the trees of the field shall yield their fruit."*

The third manifestation of the spirit in terms of water is rain. In **[Deuteronomy 11:14]**, God says, *"Then I will give you the rain for your land in its season, the early rain and the latter rain, that you may gather in your grain, your new wine, and your oil."*

God promised; I would give you rain in due season. And there are various kinds of rain in the scripture; We have the former and the latter rain in the Jewish calendar year. These are two distinct kinds of rain that produce two different results. But a lack of rain produces drought and famine as in the days of Elijah and Jezebel.

In the days of Elijah and Jezebel, there was a severing of the rain because Jezebel was building her kingdom by drawing from the resources of the Covenant People. She fed her false prophets at her table, confiscating food and benefits from Kingdom People. So, Elijah says, we are going to stop the rain. *When the rain stops, heaven is shut.*

Rain is not a favor, but it is significant because it is an open heaven. In **[2ⁿᵈ Chronicles 7:14]**, God said if you pray, seek my face, turns from your wicked ways I will heal your land. The healing of the land is directly correlated with rain falling on the land of your life. If you have iron or brass heaven, the rain of heaven is not falling upon your life. The Lord said I would send you rain in due season. *Say Lord let it rain massive blessings in every area of my live-in Jesus' Name!*

There are many places and people's lives that are steel heaven; nothing happens, nothing works, nothing opens, and nothing gives.

KEY TO OPEN YOUR CLOSED HEAVEN

Here are some keys or dynamics that can force heaven to open in your life.

1. TITHING: **[Malachi 3:10]**

2. GIVING: **[Luke 6:38]**

3. PRAYER: **[2nd Chronicles 7:14]**

4. **FASTING: [Isaiah 58]**

5. FAITH: **[Mark 11:23-24]**

6. YOUR GIFT: **[Proverbs 18:16]**

In Hosea, God said, I will send your rain in due season, in due time. Zechariah said I have prayed in the rain season for the rain to fall. Pray thus: *Lord let it rain favor, let favor come, let blessing rain, let healing rain, let deliverance rain, let prosperity come, Lord rain categorical promotion.*

When the rain of the Holy Spirit begins to fall in your life, in your ministry, in your family, and the nations, the volume and scope of revenue become unfathomable, beyond what you can measure. It is impossible, for eyes have not seen; ears have not heard...."

I prophesy God will bring rain in your life this season in Jesus' Name!

God shall displace draught out of your lives this day in Jesus' Name.

It is extremely difficult to work in dearth conditions. It is very difficult to operate in famine conditions. Because if you are in famine condition, you must have the prophetic gift to sustain your oil and flour. And many times, it is very difficult to get a credible prophetic gift that can come into your life in the season of drought and sustain what you have. But we need a prophetic mantle to break and burst the heavens open and cause rain to fall in your season.

Say, Lord! Send the rain now.

METAPHORICAL SYMBOLS OF RAIN IN SCRIPTURE

What do you think about when you see rainfall from the sky? Do you think about God's design and His gracious provision for the world? When was the last time that you thanked God for rain? *Have you ever thought of rain as being a symbol of the love of God?*

There are two main Hebrew words for rain: *"Matar"* and *"Geshem."* In the New Testament, the words used for rain are *"Broche"* and *"Photos."* In scriptures, rain is often used to symbolize a blessing from God, in both conditional blessings for obedience as well as a part of God's common grace. Other times, rain is used to punish, as in the historical narrative of Noah.

[Leviticus 26:4] *"Then I shall give you rains in their season so that the land* *will yield its produce and the trees of the field will bear their fruit."*

[Deuteronomy 32:2] *"Let my teaching fall like rain, and my words descend like dew, like showers on new grass, like abundant rain on tender plants."*

[Proverbs 16:15] *"When a king's face brightens, it means life; his favor is like a rain cloud in spring."*

God loves all His creation in a manner called common grace. God even loves those who set themselves up in enmity against Him by giving them good gifts of rain, sunshine, family, food, water, restraining evil, and other common grace elements. Just as God is generous with his enemies, so should we be. **[Matthew 5:45]** *"He makes his sun rise on the evil and the good and sends rain on the just and the unjust."*

[Luke 6:35] *"But love your enemies, do good to them, and lend to them without expecting to get anything back. Then your reward will be great, and you will be children of the Highest because he is kind to the ungrateful and wicked."*

[Acts 14:17] *"Yet he has not left himself without testimony: He has shown kindness by giving you rain from heaven and crops in their seasons; he provides you with plenty of food and fills your hearts with joy."*

RAIN CHRISTIAN QUOTES

1. *"How much of life do we miss by waiting to see the rainbow before thanking God there is rain?"*

2. *"Life isn't about waiting for the storm to pass. It's about learning how to dance in the rain."*

3. "Rain, rain, have your way because either way, God will reign."

4. "Hallelujah, grace like rain falls on me. Hallelujah, and all my stains are washed away."

FAMOUS RAIN QUOTES
COMPILED BY THE KIDADI TEAM

Here are some famous rain quotes for your edification.

1. "Let the rain kiss you. Let the rain beat upon your head with silver liquid drops. Let the rain sing you a lullaby." - **Langston Hughes.**

2. "Do not be angry with the rain; it simply does not know how to fall upwards." - **Vladimir Nabokov.**

3. "Rain is grace; rain is the sky descending to the earth;

without rain, there would be no life." - **John Updike.**

4. *"Some people walk in the rain; others just get wet."* - **Roger Miller.**

5. *"Into each life, some rain must fall; Some days must be dark and dreary."*

6. *Henry Wadsworth Longfellow.*

7. *"Life isn't about waiting for the storm to pass. It's about learning to dance in the rain."* - **Vivian Greene.**

ELIJAH THE ORACLE PRAYS FOR RAIN

[1st Kings 17:1-6]

"And Elijah the Tishbite, who was of the inhabitants of Gilead, said unto

Ahab, As the Lord God of Israel liveth, before whom I stand, there shall not be dew nor rain these years, but according to my word. And the word of the Lord came unto him, saying, Get thee hence, and turn thee eastward, and hide thyself by the brook Cherith, that is before Jordan. And it shall be, that thou shalt drink of the brook; and I have commanded the ravens to feed thee there. So, he went and did according to the word of the Lord: for he went and dwelt by the brook Cherith, that is before Jordan. And the ravens brought him bread and flesh in the morning, and bread and flesh in the evening; and he drank of the brook."

ELIJAH PRAYS FOR RAIN

[1ˢᵗ Kings 18:36-38]

Elijah told the wicked king Ahab that God would stop the rain until Elijah said so. **[1ˢᵗ Kings 17:1-6]**. He did this as a judgment upon King Ahab. When it was time, Elijah climbed to the top of Mount Carmel to pray for rain. **[1st Kings 18]**. As he prayed, he told his servant to look towards the sea for any sign of rain. Elijah prayed and trusted God to answer. He knew that God was going to keep His promise.

There are several things that we can learn from this story. No matter what situation you are in, remember that God is faithful. Like Elijah, let us listen to what God tells us to do. Not only should we listen like Elijah, but we should also follow God's commands as Elijah did. We must also not lose hope. Let us fully trust and lean upon God and believe that He will act. Let us persevere in prayer until He answers. **[1st Kings 18:41]** *"Now Elijah said to Ahab, "Go up, eat and drink; for there is the sound of the roar of a heavy shower."*

[James 5:17-18] *"Elijah was a man with a nature like ours, and he prayed earnestly that it would not rain, and it did not rain on the earth for three years and six months. Then he prayed again, and the sky poured rain, and the earth produced its fruit. My brethren, if any among you strays from the truth and one turns him back, let him know that he who turns a sinner from the error of his way will save his soul from death and will cover a multitude of sins."*

WATER OF FLOOD WASHES SIN AWAY

[Isaiah 45:8] *"Drip down, O heavens, from above, and let the clouds pour down righteousness; Let the earth open up and salvation bear fruit, And* *righteousness spring up with it. I, the Lord, have created it."*

WATER WASHES SIN AWAY

Over and over in Scripture, we are told that our sin contaminates us. Sin has contaminated the world and our flesh, and our souls. We are utterly wicked because of Adam's fall, and we need the Blood of Christ to wash us clean. God demands purity and holiness because He is completely Holy. We can see this reflected in the historical narrative of Noah and the Ark. God purified the land by drowning its inhabitants with the floodwaters so that Noah and his family could be saved. **[1st Peter 3:18-22; Genesis 7:17-24]; 2nd Peter 2:5; 2nd Peter 3:6].**

[Ezekiel 36:25] *"Then I will sprinkle clean water on you, and you will be clean; I will cleanse you from all your filthiness from all your idols."*

[Hebrews 10:22] *"Let us draw near to God with a sincere heart and with the full assurance that faith brings, having our hearts sprinkled to cleanse us from a guilty conscience and having our bodies washed with pure water."*

[1st Corinthians 6:11] *"Such were some of you, but you were washed, but you were sanctified, but you were justified in the Name of the Lord Jesus Christ and the Spirit of our God."*

WAITING ON GOD

[Isaiah 40:31] *"But they that wait upon the Lord shall renew their strength; they shall mount up with wings as eagles; they shall run, and not be weary, and they shall walk, and not faint."*

One of the hardest things in the world to do is to wait on God. We think we know what God should do and when it needs to be done. But the truth is — we only have a small inclination into what is going on. God knows all things that are and will be. We can faithfully wait on God because He has promised to do what is best for us. **[James 5:7-8]** *"Therefore be patient, brethren, until the coming of the Lord. The farmer waits for the precious produce of the soil, being patient about it until it gets the early and late rains. You also be patient. Establish your hearts, for the coming of the Lord is at hand."*

[Hosea 6:3] *"So let us know, let us press on to know the Lord. His going forth is as certain as the dawn; And He will come to us like the rain, Like the spring rain watering the earth."*

WAITING ON GOD QUOTES

"Waiting for God is not laziness. Waiting for God is not the abandonment of effort." – **UNKNOWN.**

CHAPTER SEVEN

THE RIVER METAPHOR

[Revelation 22:1-2] *"And he shewed me a pure river of water of life, clear as crystal, proceeding out of the throne of God and the Lamb. Amid the street of it, and on either side of the river, was there the tree of life, which bare twelve manners of fruits, and yielded her fruit every month: and the leaves of the tree were for the healing of the nations."*

THE RIVER METAPHOR

When we read that in God's city, there is a river, which metaphorically means *a never-ending supply of life*, it's deeply comforting. In the book of Revelation, the river runs from God's very throne, from God's presence **[Revelation 22:1-2; Ezekiel 47:1-12]**. The river of life in Revelation represents God's life-giving presence.

So, the next manifestation of the Spirit in the stead of water is Rivers. If you are like Ezekiel in **[Ezekiel 47:1-3]** and you are standing in a dry river, this means you are not anointed to do anything great; your anointing is only to stand. If the water of the Spirit does not anoint your feet, you can't walk in places you have never walked before.

If you are like Ezekiel in **[Ezekiel 47:4]** and the water is not yet at your knee level, the water of the Holy Spirit does not anoint your knees; therefore, you can't pray and get tangible results. You pray and pray but without any results.

As in **[Ezekiel 47:4]**, if the river is not up to your waist level, it means your waist is not anointed. Everything you are trying hard to produce never manifests; you experience bareness and unfruitfulness in all areas of your life. You continue to experience near success syndrome; your life becomes a life of miscarriage and abortions. *Say I reject it.*

In **[Ezekiel 47:5]** again, if you don't have enough water to swim in, you will never get to the level of swimming in prosperity; you always lack enough anointing. You are confined to a little tank, and the reference to you and your endeavor will be about your little tank. But when God opens heaven for you, and it starts raining in your life, then your rivers start breaking their banks.

RIVERS WITH HEADS METAPHOR

In **[Genesis 2]**, the rivers that flow through the Garden of Eden had four heads. Israel did not have a river with a head, so God sent them to Egypt. Egypt is to be the surrogate mother of Israel because Palestine or Canaan land could not grow a nation. It couldn't take the seed and become pregnant to grow a nation.

So, God took Joseph as the "spermer" or the seed and planted it in the womb of Egypt, and Egypt became the surrogate mother of Israel. It's artificial and metaphorical insemination. Egypt is growing this nation Israel, and the umbilical cord feeding this baby nation is the river, Nile. The river Nile is feeding this baby Israel in the womb of Egypt.

Because Israel did not control the head of the river Nile, they eventually became a slave to the system. ***Anything you cannot control in your life will enslave you.***

The Egyptian system was feeding and sustaining them until God pulled them out of Egypt and sent them to the land of promise where they now have the head of the river Jordan, with Mount Hermon, where the anointing falls, where the mechanism of thoughts and thinking and control can be, where they can cross at will and decides who can cross and when to cross.

Jericho is small in your sight because you are controlling the thought mechanism in your city, in your region. You are no longer a reactor to actors and players but a creator, a major player. You now influence the legislation; you influence government; you influence the private sector. Nobody can make a major decision in your region without checking with you first because your rivers have heads. *I pray that your rivers shall come with heads in the Name of Jesus. Amen!*

SIGNIFICANCE OF THE RIVER IN SCRIPTURE

Jesus said out of your belly shall flow rivers of living water. It will originate from within you to change the dynamics of the entire region. *But you must be smart with rivers.*

Symbolically the idea of the river in scripture *"traces the landscape"* of the history of redemption. In the garden of Eden, a river ran through the middle to irrigate the land. When God visited his wrath upon Pharaoh in Egypt, He first turned the Nile River into the blood. By turning the river to blood, God was symbolically and metaphorically demonstrating that He had put to death the Egyptian god of the river, *'Hapi,'* the Egyptian god of the river, fertility, and life.

Later, when God brought His people Israel out of Egypt, He led them across the Red Sea, through the Jordan River, and into the Promised Land. Providentially, God arranged that Jesus Christ is baptized by John in the same Jordan River, even at the very place where Israel had crossed so many centuries earlier. Scripture let us know that the spot John baptized was called *'Beth-abara,'* which means the house or place of crossing. Again, the symbolism is very rich.

During the great "feast of tabernacles," the Jews would remember the promise of a temple to come, which God' Oracle Ezekiel had spoken of in **[Ezekiel 47]**. Ezekiel foretold that a river would flow out of the temple on that day.

And in **[John 7:37-39]**, Jesus stood up amid the people celebrating that feast, who were looking for that time to come, and cried out, *"if any man thirsts let him come to me, and, as the scriptures say, 'out of his belly shall flow rivers of living water.'"*

Jesus knew exactly what He was doing. He was claiming to be that Temple which Ezekiel had spoken of, the One in whom the presence of God dwelled, and out of Whom flowed a river of life which the Old Covenant temple had only been a shadow of. And all who come to Him in faith are made part of that temple **[1st Peter 2:4-5]**, and the usefulness of the Spirit of Christ dwelling in them well up like a life-giving river.

That is why the Psalmist said that there was a *"river whose streams make glad the city of God."* **[Psalm 46:4].** Christ's fulness in His people is like a river of life, which will never run dry. This river ultimately leads us to eternal rest where there is *"a river of the water of life, flowing from the throne of God and of the Lamb through the middle of the street of the city."* Jesus offers the water of life to all who come thirsting for righteousness they know they do not have.... drink from Him and be satisfied eternally! ***Glory to God!***

RIVER QUOTES AND CREDITS

"A river cuts through rock, not because of its power, but because of its persistence." — **Jim Watkins.**

"Rivers know this: there is no hurry. We shall get there someday." — **A A Milne**

"A good river is nature's life work in song." — **Mark Helprin.**

"No one tests the depth of a river with both feet." — **Proverb.**

"Don't push the river; it will flow. Don't push the love; it will grow." — **Unknown.**

"A river is more than an amenity; it is a treasure." — **Oliver Wendell Holmes.**

"A river doesn't just carry water; it carries life." — **Amit Kalantri.**

"Intelligence is like a river: the deeper it is, the less noise it makes." — **Unknown.**

"Rivers are roads that move and carry us whither we wish to go." — **Blaise Pascal.**

"You drown not by falling into a river, but by staying submerged in it." — **Paulo Coelho.**

CHAPTER EIGHT

THE WELL METAPHOR

[Proverbs 5:15] *"Drink water from your cistern and freshwater from your well."*

Each major player in the scripture got their wife at a well. But the amazing thing about these women that were met at a well is that they were all barren but never remained barren. Isaac met Rebecca well because she was not just going to give birth to children, but her role was to birth a destiny. Rachael was met at a well, Zipporah, Moses' wife, was met at the well, and even Jesus met His bride, the Church of the gentile at the well.

In **[John Chapter 4],** Jesus was sitting at a well that Jacob did not dig; but Jacob's well was named. According to Biblical records, Jacob never dug a well. Abraham dug wells, Isaac dug wells, but there is no scripture stating a well-named Abraham's well or Isaac's well even though they dug wells.

But years later, you find Jacob, who never dug one; he now has a well named after him. Jacob's well is dug in the land that he gave Joseph. He gave Joseph a piece of land when he thought Joseph was dead for an inheritance. Even though Joseph was an enslaved person in Egypt. Joseph never had to go through the process to get his land.

The land was already given and paid for; he had the title deed of that land. And his father, Jacob, assigned him to grow seed for the future generation and dug a well on that land. *Wells represents generational blessing. You must have a well in your life because it is a generational blessing.*

In **[John 4],** when Jesus was at a well in Samaria, a woman comes out of the city; this is a prototype of the bride of Christ, the church. She is a Samaritan, meaning she is partly Gentile and partly Jew. She represents the Old Testament and the New Testament. And Jesus says to her; you've been married five times. She was married to five dispensations before Jesus got there. *The dispensation of conscience, human, government, promise, and the law.* But all those husbands could not make her pregnant. And He said to her, the one you are living with right now, you are not even married to him. That is grace because grace was not yet given. All the stuff in the past couldn't get her pregnant, but a generational seed seating by the well was a generational blessing. Because here is a well dug and drawn from for two thousand years and never ran dry.

When we interact with wells, we have, for example, Joseph's brothers; they threw Joseph in a dry well. That was significant because they were dry people, they were not generational people, they didn't think of the future, they didn't understand that Joseph was not a family man; Joseph was a global man.

And so, their small-mindedness and their foolish thinking made them throw him in the well. This was indicative of their small-mindedness because their well was dry. If they had enough sense, they would have put their money together and paid for Joseph to go to business school in Egypt because Joseph has a global anointing, not a family church.

When Joseph was taken out of the well, God blessed Joseph by sending another agency that had the sense to develop long-distance transportation. To move the gift from one place to another. Israel was still following sheep, while the Ishmaelites have developed modern transportation. A long-distance transportation system that can withstand any adversity in the desert, which Joseph was placed on. He was given an economy class ticket to Egypt. So he can begin his schooling. So, he can rule the world in the years to come.

You must dig it deep to last generationally when digging a well. **[Isaiah 12:3]** says, *"Therefore with joy, you will draw water from the wells of salvation."*

[Isaiah 54:1] said, *"sing O barren, so if you are in a barren situation right now and your wells are dried, you must be able to sing Babe sing."*

Singing is not just being melodious or harmonious; singing is an attitude of minds, you don't have to carry a tune, but you must have the ability to address some things in a dry season. Singing increases the water table in your life; if the water level is low, you cannot sustain life at ground level.

God promised Israel to take you to a land with copious wells that you did not dig. When God gives you wells, you didn't dig; it means He has eliminated the process. **[Luke 6:38]** *"Give and it will be given to you: good* *measure, pressed down, shaken together, and running over will be put into your bosom. For with the same measure that you use, it will be measured back to you."*

In **[Luke 16:19-31],** the rich man and Lazarus are in two different worlds altogether. When Lazarus dies, he goes to Abraham's bosom, so the bosom then is the place of wealth. So, when men give to your bosom, they give toward your wealthy place. When a baby is born, you don't give it T-bone steak and chili soup. You take the baby and place the baby at the wealthy place, the bosom, and breastfeed the baby.

Here is the principle of this metaphor: an outside organization eats the meat, chew the hamburger and fried rice, process all of that, and deposit the nutrient in the wealthy place [the breast]. All the baby does is come to the wealthy place and suck. In other words, for the baby, the process has been eliminated.

In **[Genesis 22]**, Abraham will access a new level of blessing. He said to his boys, *'wait here, and the lad Isaac and I will worship The Lord!'* They climbed to the top of the hill; Abraham was about to kill his son Isaac. And the angel of the Lord says they don't take your son's life; he said look behind you there is a ram tied in the thicket.

Again, here is the principal metaphor: Abraham passed his blessing on the way up; he didn't even know there was a blessing because he had not accessed a level of the Spirit. He didn't even recognize his blessing on the way up, but when he turned around at the age of 120 years and saw his blessing, its horns by thorns tied the ram.

The ram's horns are used for defense, so God was saying metaphorically to Abraham at the age of 120 years, at your age, to go through the process of chasing your blessings around the mountain will be too much for you. So, I will take the fight out of your blessing; I am taking the struggle out of your life. I will take sorrow out of your life; the blessings of the Lord maketh rich and added no sorrow to it. *I decree! If you have been weeping for too long now, God is taking the weeping out of your blessing. Weeping will endure for the night but today is your day of joy in the Name of Jesus Christ. Amen!*

God is eliminating the fight from the things you have fought for all these years!

This day God is taking the fight out of your blessing.

The devil program certain people to fight for everything they have.

You must fight for your name, fight for your dignity and integrity, fight for your money and property, fight for a used car, fight for your space, fight for air, but the devil.

God is saying in this your hour, this is your season, it will be quick, He is eliminating the process, and He is taking the fight out of your blessings generationally in the Name of Jesus Christ. Amen!

Generational wells are wells you didn't dig; time and season will not affect the water tables. It will not be a temporary well; it will be a well that will bless you generationally. Two thousand years going, your great, great-grandsons and daughters are going to meet their spouse coming out of a city seating at your well, Jacob's well.

Take your time, brethren, dig deep that well, plan generationally, plan for your great-grandchildren, and put money aside for their future, even before they are born. Place your thought on the future and dig a generational well. Get into your desert and dig a well, Jehoshaphat the water will flow. Moses, the Red Sea, will open for you, Joshua, the wall of Jericho, is coming down, David the Goliath is dying today in the Name of Jesus Christ!

WATER WELL QUOTES

"Men can dig wells, but they can't create water." "After digging a thousand wells of my own and stumbling upon a thousand others dug by the hands of thirsty men, I have yet to realize that the only well that can satiate every thirst is the one *that men will never dig."* – **UNKNOWN**

THE SEA AND THE BIBLE

[Matthew 13:47-50] *"Again, the kingdom of heaven is like, unto a net, that was cast into the sea, and gathered of every kind: Which, when it was full, they drew to shore, and sat down, and gathered the good into vessels, but cast the bad away. So shall it be at the end of the world: the angels shall come forth, and sever the wicked from among the just, and shall cast them into the furnace of fire: there shall be wailing and gnashing of teeth."*

SEA AND THE BIBLE

The next manifestation of the spirit in terms of water is the sea. What does the Bible say about Sea as Symbol? In the fourth pair of the parables of **[Matthew 13],** Jesus instructs His disciples apart from the general multitude He had spoken to earlier. The seventh parable in the chapter, the Parable of the Dragnet in **[verse 47]**, teaches that in the metaphoric church, the good and evil who intermingle on earth will be completely separated *"at the end of the age."*

This set time of separation will be, for good, a time of rejoicing in a bright, eternal future, but for the evil, it will be a time of mourning before eternal oblivion. In **[Matthew 4:18-20]**, Jesus says to Peter and Andrew, *"Follow Me, and I will make you fishers of men,"* providing a partial interpretation of this parable.

When Jesus Christ later made the twelve disciples fishers of men, they went out and brought in "catches" of converts. Thus, the professing church, composed of the "called," are caught in God's net, which His servants draw in.

Peter, Andrew, James, and John had been fishermen before their calling, so the idea of the dragnet was a familiar and vivid picture to them. Their work entailed using a net - a dragnet - of great length, weighted by lead and designed to sweep the bottom of the sea, gathering fish in masses. Two boats would drag this net between them, sweeping a section of the Sea of Galilee, after which the sailors would haul the net to shore. The fishers would go through the entire net there, keeping the good fish but burning the substandard ones to avoid catching them later.

The symbol of "the sea" is like the beasts rising out of the sea and out of the earth **[Revelation 13:1, Revelation 13:11]**. It designates origination, representing the realm of the earth. Christ's origin is the realm of heaven, but the beasts, part of a corrupt system, come from the sea and the earth. The sea, a body of water, symbolizes *"peoples, multitudes, nations, and tongues"* **[Revelation 17:15].**

In the parable, when the fish are caught in a net thrown in the sea, Jesus signifies that members of His church are "the called" out of the world **[Romans 1:5-6; Romans 8:28].**

The dragnet gathers some of every kind; God's net catches fish without partiality to age, sex, race, ethnicity, class, wealth, intelligence, language, beauty, and so forth. His interest is in developing our character and whether He can work with us **[Romans 2:11; Romans 5:8; Romans 9:18, Romans 9:21].**

THE SEA METAPHOR OF THE SPIRIT

[Psalm 95:5] *"The sea is His, for it was He who made it, and His hands formed the dry land."*

And there are two types of seas in the scriptures: the freshwater sea and saltwater sea. Freshwater sea is revelation knowledge that comes out of a process; it is sequential revelation knowledge. For example, if I say **one, two, three, four,** the next sequence will be **five.** But If I say **two, four, six,** and the next in the sequence will be **eight**. The next sequence will be fifteen if I say three, six, nine, and twelve.

So, there is an obvious sequence when dealing with freshwater seas. That is sequential revelation knowledge. It is knowledge by experience; it is good counsel from the council and counselors. It is knowledge by maturity. This kind f knowledge comes as God begins to lead you from one role and room to another. God told Elijah to anoint Elisha, not in your place but your room.

Jesus said to His disciples after he fed 5000 people. So, they will now walk in the next sequence of revelation knowledge.

The problems we have in Churches are not a lack of the presence of the Gospel of Christ but a lack of quality. The message is deficient and inadequate. We have so many people saved, but then what next? Many people are saved but are deficient because the sequence of development and growth is not sequential. The process of the Gospel in many churches and ministries is designed to keep you in one place with no growth. Do not pass go, do not collect $200. You stay in square one, like a monopoly game. That is why there must be the manifestation of the metaphor of the sea of the Holy Spirit where we have sequential revelation knowledge leading to categorical growth.

In the scripture, you have the saltwater sea. If you drink salt water without diluting it, it will mess up your brain because this level of revelation knowledge comes directly from heaven. It cannot be received directly. It must be broken down into bite-sized pieces for those willing to receive it. And you can only receive that kind of revelation knowledge according to your capacity.

Moses had this capacity. When he stretched forth his rod across the Red Sea, he was accessing raw knowledge that no one else had ever seen, and that is evidence; when God gave him the entire creative forum in the Old Testament, the creative process was given to Moses by God because he had access to raw revelation knowledge. And raw revelation knowledge is timeless.

There are three measurements of time in the scripture:

I. **Chronos:** that is the unfolding of time,

II. **The second one is Kairos, when God does something, brings** favor, and changes destiny.

III. **But then you have the spirit time.**

The spirit realm is a timeless zone where *the past, the present, and the future* are all in one zone. So, when Moses entered this timeless zone of raw revelation knowledge, he saw the end from the beginning. He had a great understanding of what God was going to do. And the great thing about being in the spirit of the timeless zone is divine acceleration by tapping into the knowledge of seas, by tapping into the knowledge of God's timeless zone. ***I decree that you are entering a dimension of tremendous acceleration in the Name of Jesus Christ. Amen!***

The Syrophoenician woman got the timelessness dimension. She said to Jesus; please heal my daughter, and Jesus said I can't heal your daughter because it is not yet your time. So, what she had to do was to enter the zone of timelessness.

And Jesus said I couldn't give you the bread meant for the children of Israel. The children of Israel are in a certain time. That is, this person is allocated this bread at this time. She said I know that the bread is given to these children at this time, but we are entitled to crumbles that fall from the children's table or of that time.

So, she took her daughter out of a time when she was depraved and deprived and thrust the girl into the dimension of timelessness, and everything is now in the zone of timelessness.

Jesus had to amend His job description and heal that girl by accelerating her time. *It is your own time now! God is accelerating things in your time, in your life now. You never thought it could happen to you, but it will. In the next few weeks, God will accelerate some things for you; things you could not do in years, you would do them in weeks and days. We need a revelation and a revolution like that in the body of Christ. This is the kingdom of God.*

SEA, METAPHORIC BIBLE REFERENCE

[Isaiah 57:20] *"**But the wicked are like the tossing sea,** for it cannot be quiet, and its waters toss up refuse and mud."*

[Isaiah 17:12] *"**Alas, the uproar of many peoples Who roar like the roaring of the seas**, and the rumbling of nations **Who** rush on like the rumbling of mighty waters!"*

[James 1:6] *"But he must ask in faith without any doubting, for the one who **doubts is like the surf of the sea,** driven and tossed by the wind."*

[Isaiah 48:18] *"If only you had paid attention to My commandments! Then your well-being would have been like a river, **and your righteousness like the waves of the sea.**"*

SEA QUOTES

"The sea does not like to be restrained." – Rick Riordan

"The cure for anything is saltwater: sweat, tears or the sea." – Isak Dinesen

"Sometimes in the waves of change, we find our true direction." – Unknown

"A rising tide lifts all boats." – Sean Lemass

"How inappropriate to call this planet Earth when it is Ocean." – Arthur C. Clarke

"A smooth sea never made a skilled sailor." – Franklin D. Roosevelt.

"Family is a life jacket in the stormy sea of life." – J.K. Rowling.

"Life's roughest storms prove the strength of our anchors." – Unknown.

CHAPTER NINE

OPERATIONS OF THE SPIRIT

This chapter shall deal briefly with the seven operational phases, facets, or manifestations of the Holy Spirit in the Believer's life. These are the seven facets or manifestations of the Holy Spirit in the believer's life:

1. THE HOLY SPIRIT IS THE SPIRIT OF JUSTICE

The Spirit of Justification: *"........you were justified in the Name of the Lord Jesus Christ and by **the Spirit of our God.**"* We are all justified because of God's grace and by our faith in the finished work of Christ Jesus. And it is the Spirit of God, the Holy Spirit, who draws us and empowers us to acknowledge Jesus Christ as our Lord and Savior.

[1st Corinthians 12:3]. *This is the first work of the Spirit when one is born again.*

2. THE HOLY SPIRIT IS THE SPIRIT OF SANCTIFICATION

The Spirit of Sanctification: *"...God from the beginning chose you for salvation through **sanctification by the Spirit** and belief in the truth."* **[2nd Thessalonians 2:13].** Sanctification is the process of God's grace by which the believer is separated from sin, purified by a life lived in the Spirit. **[Galatians 5:16, Galatians 5:25, and Romans 8:1-14].** *The fruit of the Spirit will begin to manifest as we yield to the process of sanctification.*

3. THE HOLY SPIRIT IS THE SPIRIT OF LIFE

The Spirit of Life: *"For the law of the **Spirit of life** in Christ Jesus has made me free from the law of sin and death."* **[Romans 8:2]**. The Spirit of life is the Spirit of adoption **[Romans 8:15]** which makes us sons and daughters of God **[Romans 8:16-19]**. We can now live in the resurrection power of Jesus Christ, where the operations of the gifts of the Spirit cause our lives to become supernatural. The Spirit gives life to our mortal bodies. Healing and strength come into our bodies **[Romans 8:11),** as well as giving us a glorified body for eternity.

4. THE HOLY SPIRIT IS THE SPIRIT OF TRUTH

The Spirit of Truth: *"**The Spirit of truth,** whom the world cannot receive because it neither sees Him nor* knows Him; but you know Him, for He dwells with you and will be in you." **[John 14:17]**. It is the known truth that sets free! The truth will set us free and bring **revelation knowledge** as the Holy Spirit teaches us. The Spirit of truth will reveal Jesus to us **[John 15:26]**. And divinely inspired vision will be given to lead us into all truth and reveal the kingdom to us; not 'Tunnel Visions'; not Deceptions. Deception will be removed, and the lies destroyed by *the Spirit of Truth.*

5. THE HOLY SPIRIT IS THE SPIRIT OF WISDOM

The Spirit of Wisdom: *"That the God of our Lord Jesus Christ, the Father of glory, may give you the **Spirit of wisdom** and revelation in the knowledge of Him."* **[Ephesians 1:17]**. Not only will the Spirit give us a deeper knowledge of Jesus, but it will also give us insight into His mind and what He is doing in our dispensation **[1st Corinthians 2:6-16]**. The Holy Spirit is our teacher **[John 14:25-26]**.

6. THE HOLY SPIRIT IS THE SPIRIT OF DELIVERANCE

The Spirit of Deliverance: *"But if I cast out demons by the **Spirit of God**, surely the kingdom of God has come upon you."* **[Matthew 12:28]**. It is by the power of the Holy Spirit that we are delivered from sin, and by that same Spirit, demons are cast out, and the powers of darkness are defeated.

7. THE HOLY SPIRIT IS OUR PRAYER HELPER

The Spirit of Prayer: *"Likewise, the Spirit also helps in our weaknesses. For we do not know what we should pray for as we ought, but the **Spirit Himself makes intercession** for us with groanings which cannot be uttered."* **[Romans 8:26]**.

Ephesians 6:18 tells us that all prayer should be done in the Spirit.

These are the seven profound works that the Holy Spirit will do in our lives. And can be developed for a separate Book. If we allow Him to do these works in and through us, He will perfect us.

There are other names of the Holy Spirit in Scripture, which, however, will all identify one aspect or the other with the seven listed operational functions of the Holy Spirit. Such as the Spirit of holiness, the spirit burning, the Spirit of faith, which we shall briefly examine in the next chapter.

HOLY SPIRIT QUOTES

"God sent Jesus as an example to see if we could retain and maintain the Holy Spirit in human flesh. – **Benny Hinn**.

"The same Holy Spirit who implants faith within a life implant the boldness to verbalize that faith." - **Alistair Begg**

Had the Holy Spirit not been with Jesus, He would have sinned." - **Benny Hinn**

Earthly wisdom is doing what comes naturally. Godly wisdom is doing what the Holy Spirit compels us to do." - **Charles Stanley**.

CHAPTER TEN

ENCOUNTER WITH THE SPIRIT OF FAITH

"And since we have the same spirit of faith, according to what is written, "I believed, and therefore I spoke," we also believe and therefore speak." **[2nd Corinthians 4:13].**

The Spirit of faith is one of the components of the Holy Spirit, and it is the same from one generation to another. From diverse testimonies in scriptures, we discover that the Spirit of faith is the master key to a world of unlimited possibilities.

Concerning the heroes of faith in scriptures, the Bible records: *"Who through subdued faith kingdoms, worked righteousness, obtained promises, stopped the mouths of lions, quenched the violence of fire, escaped the edge of the sword, out of weakness were made strong, became valiant in battle, turned to flight the armies of the aliens."* **[Hebrews 11:33-34].**

So, the Spirit of faith establishes our dominion over the earth's overall situations and circumstances.

It is important to recognize that we require the Spirit of faith to fulfill our glorious destiny in Christ. That is because our human imagination cannot handle the exploits that God will work in our lives. Hence, we need the Spirit of faith to comprehend and actualize them.

Moreover, this Spirit quenches all the devil's fiery darts and deals with the issues that confront us as God takes us from one level to another. From glory to glory!

That is why craving and desiring the Spirit of faith is vital to fulfilling our glorious destiny in Christ **[Ephesians 6:16]**. *"Above all, taking the shield of faith with which, you will be able to quench all the fiery darts of the wicked one."*

[Romans 1:17] *"For in it, the righteousness of God is revealed from faith to faith; as it is written, "The just shall live by faith."*

THE SPIRIT OF FAITH UNIQUENESS

1. THE SPIRIT OF FAITH EMPOWERS US TO BELIEVE ALL THINGS:

Apostle Paul said, in **[Acts 24:14]** *"But this I confess to you, that according* *to the Way which they call a sect, so I worship the God of my fathers, believing all things which are written in the Law and the Prophets."*

It takes the Spirit of faith to believe all things Biblical. And we are empowered to become what we believe: *"But as many as received Him, to them He gave the right, power, authority or privilege to become children of God, to those who believe in His Name:"* **[John 1:12]**

[Mark 9:23] *"Jesus said to him, "If you can believe, all things are possible to him who believes."*

[John 14:12] *"Most assuredly, I say to you, he who believes in Me, the works that I do he will also do; and greater works than these he will do, because I go to My Father."*

It is important to understand that the spirit of fear cannot survive where the Spirit of faith dwells. So, the level to which the Spirit of faith is at work in our lives determines what God does in our lives. As it is written: *"Blessed is she who believed, for there will be a fulfillment of those things which were told her from the Lord."* **[Luke 1:45].**

2. THE SPIRIT OF FAITH IS A SPEAKING FAITH:

The Spirit of faith speaks the unspeakable through us to commit God to intervene. Jesus said: *"for it is not you who speak, but the Spirit of your Father who speaks in you."* **[Matthew 10:20].**

[2nd Corinthians 4:13] *"And since we have the same spirit of faith, according to what is written, "I believed, and therefore I spoke," we also believe and therefore speak."*

The Spirit of faith also speaks through us with what our hearts cannot conceive. For example: in **[Daniel 3:8-18]** when Shadrach, Meshach, and Abednego determined not to bow to King Nebuchadnezzar's image, I believe they were not the ones who spoke but the Spirit of Faith.

So, the Spirit of faith speaks through us to establish God's plan and purpose for our lives.

3. THE SPIRIT OF FAITH IS AN EVER-WINNING SPIRIT:

No matter the intensity of the battle, the Spirit of faith remains an ever-winning Spirit. For example, the Red Sea parted through the Spirit of faith, and the Israelites walked on the dry ground **[Exodus 14:10-30]**.

And, in the wilderness, they were supernaturally fed two meals per day

[Exodus 16:1-21]. *" So, they gathered it every morning, every man according to his need. And when the sun became hot, it melted."*

4. THE SPIRIT OF FAITH LAUNCHES US INTO THE REALM OF PEACE:

The Spirit of faith brings us to a place or into a realm of inexplicable rest, which is the platform for erupting signs and wonders. As it is written: *"For we who have believed do enter that rest, as He has said: "So I swore in My wrath, 'They shall not enter My rest,'" although the works were finished from the foundation of the world."* **[Hebrews 4:3]**.

It is also written: *"There remains, therefore, a rest for the people of God. For he who has entered His rest has himself also ceased from his works as God did from His. 11 Let us, therefore, be diligent to enter that rest, lest anyone fall according to the same example of disobedience."* **[Hebrews 4:9-11].**

The state of rest is the platform for divine intervention. And it is the Spirit of faith that brings us into that realm of unperturbed rest: *"Be still and know that I am God; I will be exalted among the nations, I will be exalted in the earth!"* **[Psalm 46:10].**

"The Lord will fight for you, and you shall hold your peace." **[Exodus 14:14]**

[Psalm 23:5-6] *"You prepare a table before me in the presence of my enemies; you anoint my head with oil; my cup runs over. Surely goodness and mercy shall follow me all the days of my life, and I will dwell in the house of the Lord forever."*

[Psalm 110:1-2] *"The Lord said to my Lord, "Sit at My right hand, till I make Your enemies Your footstool." The*

Lord shall send the rod of Your strength out of Zion. Rule amid Your enemies."

[Ruth 3:18] *"Then she said, "Sit still, my daughter, until you know how the matter will turn out, for the man will not rest until he has concluded the matter this day."*

KEYS TO REST IN THE SPIRIT:

[2ⁿᵈ Chronicles 32:8] *"With him is an arm of flesh; but with us is the Lord our God, to help us and to fight our battles." And the people were strengthened by the words of Hezekiah king of Judah."*

Here are some pointers to divine rest.

- ➤ The key to rest in life is to rest in the Word.

- ➤ Rest of mind proceeds from rest in the Word.

- So, to access absolute rest in life, you must rest absolutely on the Word of God.

- God's Word is tested and proven; those who rest upon it cannot be shaken.

- Men are troubled because they haven't found the Word to rest upon it.

- It would help if you rested upon the Word to find rest in the world.

5. THE SPIRIT OF FAITH UNLEASHES DIVERSE SUPERNATURAL MANIFESTATIONS:

Jesus said: *"Most assuredly, I say to you, he who believes in Me, the works that I do he will also do; and greater works than these he will do because I go to My Father."* **[John 14:12].**

[John 6:28-29] *"Then they said to Him, "What shall we do, that we may work the works of God?" Jesus answered and said to them, "This is the work of God, which you believe in Him whom He sent."*

When we operate in the realm of the Spirit of faith, we operate at God's frequency, thereby commanding signs, wonders, and diverse miracles.

We must also note that the Spirit of faith is a transferable virtue and can be transferred from generation to generation. For example, Elisha said that *"the spirit of Elijah doth rest on Elisha."* **[2nd Kings 2:15].**

Therefore, we can be imparted with the Spirit of faith.

[Luke 1:17] *"He will also go before Him in the spirit and power of Elijah, 'to turn the hearts of the fathers to the children,' and the disobedient to* *the wisdom of the just, to make ready a people prepared for the Lord."*

[2nd Timothy 1:5] *"When I call to remembrance the genuine faith that is in you, which dwelt first in your grandmother Lois and your mother Eunice, and I am persuaded in you also."*

The Bibles say: *"But earnestly desire and zealously cultivate the greatest and best gifts and graces (the higher gifts and the choicest graces). And yet I will show you a still more excellent way [one that is better by far and the highest of them all—love]."* **[1st Corinthians 12:31 AMP]**.

And this faith works by Love. **[Galatians 5:6]**.

Moreover, we are admonished in scriptures to earnestly contend for the faith which was once delivered to the saints **[Jude 1:3]** *"Beloved, while I* *was very diligent to write to you concerning our common salvation, I found it necessary to write to you exhorting you to contend earnestly for the faith which was once for all delivered to the saints."*

ENCOUNTER THE SPIRIT OF FAITH?

1. THROUGH A GENUINE THIRST:

"O God, You are my God; early will I seek You; my soul thirsts for You; my flesh longs for You in a dry and thirsty land where there is no water." "So, I have looked for You in the sanctuary to see Your power and Your glory." **[Psalm 63:1-2].**

Every empowerment of the Spirit demands a desperate thirst, a longing, and a panting. As it is written: *"For I will pour water on him who is thirsty and floods on the dry ground; I will pour My Spirit on your descendants, And My blessing on your offspring; they will spring up among the grass like willows by the watercourses.'* **[Isaiah 44:3-4].**

Therefore, we must desperately desire an encounter with the Spirit of faith before we can experience the impartation.

2. THROUGH THE WORD OF GOD:

We must understand that it is not enough to possess the Spirit of faith. We must have a responsibility to keep that faith Spirit alive and working in our lives. That is because it is a living virtue, and as such, it must be adequately fed by the Word. **[Romans 10:17].**

The Spirit of faith can be likened to a bonfire, which must be fed with wood to keep it alive and high.

Thus, we keep the bonfire of the Spirit of faith alive via God's Word. The Bible says: *"And the fire on the altar shall be kept burning on it; it shall not be put out. And the priest shall burn wood on it every morning and lay the burnt offering in order on it; and he shall burn on it the fat of the peace offerings. A fire shall always be burning on the altar; it shall never go out."* **[Leviticus 6:12-13].**

When we do not feed the Spirit of faith, we starve and grieve it, and if we are not careful, it may be quenched. The Spirit of faith is a kind of spiritual aircraft that must be maintained, or it will be grounded. So, no Word-lazy believer can sustain the operation of the Spirit of faith because it draws its strength from the Word.

We must also know that the Spirit of faith is one of the best gifts of the

Spirit. That is because it puts us in command of the issue of life, which is of concern to others. This makes the Spirit of faith our strength and stays in the days of battle. **[1ˢᵗ Corinthians 12:1-11]**.

[Romans 12:6] *"Having then gifted differing according to the grace that is given to us, let us use them: if prophecy, let us prophesy in proportion to our faith."*

[TLB] *"God has given each of us the ability to do certain things well. So, if God has given you the ability to prophesy, then prophesy whenever you can—as often as your faith is strong enough to receive a message from God."*

We must also understand that the Spirit of faith is unquenchable by evil and the forces of darkness because it is ever in charge of situations and circumstances. However, it is important to understand that faith is no cheap talk; it is hard work. Therefore, we must take personal responsibility to keep the Spirit of faith alive and working in our lives by constantly feeding on the word of God daily.

I pray that you receive a fresh baptism of the Spirit of faith in Jesus' Name. Amen!

PROPHETIC PRAYERS

1. *I decree that your life becomes an ever-winning life!*

2. *The last battle you lost is the last one you will ever lose in the Name of Jesus Christ.*

3. *Everything about you becomes a sign and a wonder!*

4. *Every curse of the wicked against you averted!*

5. *An end has come to all forms of financial struggles!*

6. *The finger of the enemy will not be traceable in you!*

7. *Thank God for answered prayers!*

CHAPTER ELEVEN

--- ★ ---

THE SPIRIT OF WISDOM

*[Isaiah 11:1-4] "And there shall come forth a rod out of the stem of Jesse, and a Branch shall grow out of his roots: And the spirit of the L*ORD *shall rest upon him, the spirit of wisdom and understanding, the spirit of counsel and might, the spirit of knowledge and the fear of the LORD. And shall make him of quick understanding in fear of the L*ORD*: and he shall not judge after the sight of his eyes, neither reprove after the hearing of his ears: But with righteousness shall he judge the poor*

and reprove with equity for the meek of the earth: and he shall smite the earth: with the rod of his mouth, and with the breath of his lips shall he slay the wicked."

UNDERSTANDING THE SPIRIT OF WISDOM

Apostle Joshua Suleman said, in one of His teachings, he said: *"Behind any uncommon result is the manifestation of the Spirit of Wisdom."*

And I concur because it will take more than a sincere heart to excel in any and every area of life. It takes wisdom to excel in life. It takes God's wisdom dimension to bring results beyond the realm of sense and science. After this chapter, you shall understand the premise of the Spirit of wisdom and how to access Divine wisdom by the Spirit of God.

The Spirit of wisdom is a major dimension of the operation of the Spirit of God. Wisdom is a principal requirement for the journey of life according to **[Proverbs 4:7]**. Wisdom is crucial for life and destiny.

The Spirit of wisdom is critical that the Father, the Son, and the Holy Spirit identify with wisdom. In these passages **[Romans 16:2-7; 1st Corinthians 1:24; Isaiah 11:2; 1st Corinthians 1:30; Ephesians 1:16-17]** to mention a few.

PERSONALITIES IN SCRIPTURE THAT WALKED IN WISDOM:

1. *Moses:* By divine wisdom: Moses wrote the first five books of the Bible by the wisdom of God.

2. *Solomon* [1st Kings 3:10-13]

3. *Joshua* [Deuteronomy 34:9]

4. *Daniel* [Daniel 5:11]

5. *David* [2nd Samuel 14:20]

6. *Apostle Paul* [2nd Peter 3:15]

Wisdom affects us daily. It affects our marital choices, our financial decisions, productivity at the place of work, how we use our time, and everything else. But not just sensual and worldly wisdom but God's wisdom. Divine wisdom.

WHAT IS THE WISDOM OF GOD?

The Wisdom of God is supernatural access to life's answers and solutions **[Luke 2:47-48; Mark 6:2; Genesis 41:34-40]**. Life is full of questions, but God is full of answers, and we access the answers to the questions of life through the wisdom of God. When a man has answers from God, it is called the Wisdom of God.

The Wisdom of God is access to and application of revelational light and insight from Scripture **[Matthew 7:24-25; Luke 11:49; Jeremiah 8:9]**. The Wisdom of God reveals unto us from Scripture what others can't see and empowers us to apply it correctly. The Wisdom of God has applied revelation. The Word of the Lord is the Container of the Wisdom of God. It is access to supernatural creativity and artistry **[Exodus 28:3; Exodus 31:1-6; Psalm 104:24; Jeremiah 10:12; Proverbs 3:19]**.

The Wisdom of God is supernatural access to profitable actions steps **[Ecclesiastes 10:10; 1st Kings 3:16-28]**.

The wisdom of God guarantees a profit. The wisdom of God assists in living profitably. The wisdom of God helps to know the best decision to take within a given set of options.

The Wisdom of God is supernatural access to Divine mysteries and hidden secrets **[Job 15:8; Daniel 2:19-22 and 30]**. It gives access to the secrets of God, and the secrets of God give you access to success in life **[Job 29:4]**.

The wisdom of God gives you access to mysteries, and when you have access to mysteries, you end miseries and step into mastery. The Wisdom of God grants us supernatural access to Divine direction and guidance **[John 6:6; Proverbs 3:19]**. Wisdom knows the way to go in life, knowing what to do to get the desired results. When the wisdom of God is with you, you don't put your money in the wrong business. For the unwise, every door is a door, but not every door is for the wise. For the unwise, every opening is a breakthrough, but for the wise, some openings are traps, and it takes the wisdom of God to understand what a breakthrough is and what will break your life down. Direction brings acceleration. The wisdom of God is what delivers people.

The Wisdom of God is the superior mentality and supernatural sensibility **[Isaiah 11:3; Daniel 1:19-20]**. The wisdom of God is what makes a person many times higher than their contemporaries. The wisdom of God places people in a class of their own. It imparts us the ability to anticipate and prepare for the future **[Genesis 41:34-40; Proverbs 22:3; Proverbs 27:12]**. It imparts the ability for proactive living instead of reactive living.

The Wisdom of God is supernatural access to God's will, plan, and purpose **[Isaiah 55:8-9; Jeremiah 29:11]**. It makes us spend time in the right endeavor and not wasteful endeavors; it will help you know whom to spend the rest of your life with.

The Wisdom of God is supernatural access to Divine inspiration and ideas **[Genesis 30:37-43; Job 32:8; John 6:6]**. It ushers us into the realm of life-changing, world-governing, frustration-destroying, and wealth-creating ideas.

The Wisdom of God is a supernatural ability for witty inventions **[Proverbs 8:12; 1st Chronicles 23:5; 2nd Samuel 14:20]**. The Wisdom of God establishes people in the realm of inventions and ideas. You bring about inventions that never existed before. The Wisdom of God imparts the ability to complications and dissolve puzzles **[Daniel 5:12; John 8:2-11]**. Through the Wisdom of God, what was once complex becomes simple and what was once a puzzle becomes unraveled.

WISDOM QUOTE

"Wisdom Quotes. "It is better to remain silent at the risk of being thought a fool than to talk and remove all doubt of it."

"The fool doth think he is wise, but the wise man knows himself to be a fool.". "Whenever you find yourself on the side of the majority, it is time to reform (or pause and reflect)."

- UNKNOWN

PRAYERS

1. *Father, thank You for Your Word. To You be all the glory Lord, in Jesus' Name.*

2. *Father, I receive wisdom today in Jesus' Name.*

3. *Father, everything you have in mind for me today, I ask that it be established and everything that the devil has in store for me, let it be frustrating.*

4. *Father, I receive my total release and liberty now.*

5. *I prophesy the release of wisdom like upon my life.*

6. *I take authority over the spirit of depression and discouragement!*

7. *That satanic project against my life, family, and destiny has just been terminated!*

8. *Every demonic arrow fired into my life is refired back to sender!*

9. Everything the devil has taken and stolen from me, I decree restoration!

10. The wisdom of God shall give to me all that is mine in Jesus' Name

11. The plan of the devil for my life shall not succeed

12. A life-changing idea that will change my life for good is coming my way.

13. An inspiration that will put my name as a major key player in this generation is coming my way.

14. A life-changing idea that will change my own life is coming my way.

CHAPTER TWELVE

HOLY SPIRIT ENCOUNTER

[Acts 1:8] *"But ye shall receive power, after that the Holy Ghost has come upon you: and ye shall be witnesses unto me both in Jerusalem, and in all Judaea, and Samaria, and unto the uttermost part of the earth."*

HOLY SPIRIT ENCOUNTER

The holy spirit is the person and power of God. It is impossible to serve God effectively without the person of the Holy Spirit having a relationship and fellowship with us. The Holy Spirit is a Person. He is one

Person of the Godhead. We have God the Father, the Son, and the Holy Spirit **[1st John 5:7, Mathew 28:19-20]**.

The Father is the Almighty God, The Son is our Lord Jesus Christ, and The Holy Spirit is the one that Jesus sent to us **[Acts 1:8]**. The Holy Spirit is the carrier of God's presence and power. In **[Genesis 1:1-2]**, we see that God began to recreate the whole world through His Spirit. Jesus could not have fulfilled His ministry on earth without the Holy Spirit, **[Acts 10:38]**, tells us that God empowered Him with the Holy Spirit and Power to do great miracles. The Holy Spirit is not the Power of God; the Holy Spirit carries the Power of God. As a Christian, you cannot manifest or feel God's presence without the Holy Spirit; it is the Holy Spirit that separates Christianity from every other religion in the world. Let's look at some Characteristics of the Holy Spirit.

1. **Salvation**: The Holy Spirit is the Lord of the Harvest of Souls. **[Matthew 9:38]**. The Holy Spirit convicts sinners of their sins; one cannot be born again without the Holy Spirit. The Holy Spirit is the author of our salvation.

2. **Godliness**: The Holy Spirit enables us to live a holy and righteous life. Just as He convicts sinners of their sins, He also convicts believers of their righteousness **[John 16:8-9]**. The Holy Spirit helps us serve God in words and deeds; you cannot live right before God by your human strength, the arm of flesh will always fail you, but you must constantly depend on the Holy Spirit to live a godly life. *Remember, it's not by power, nor by might, but by my, Spirit says the Lord,* **[Zechariah 4:6]**.

3. **Supernatural**: We command the Supernatural through the Holy Spirit inside us. Through the power of the Holy Spirit, we can heal the sick, raise the dead, cast out devils, etc. We can control events from the realms of the spirit through the power of the Holy Ghost. **[Mark 16:17-18]**.

4. **Answered Prayers**: The Holy Spirit helps us pray **[Romans 8:26-27]**. The holy spirit gives us utterances in our prayers. The Holy Spirit in us guarantees answers to our prayers. He is our advocate before God. Learn to pray in the Holy Ghost, **[Jude 1:20]**.

5. **Direction**: It is the voice of the Spirit in us that gives us direction. The holy spirit is our helper; as a believer, get to know the person of the Holy Spirit.

He will guide you and teach you all things you need to know. Jesus said He would even bring back to you things you may have forgotten. The Holy Spirit is our teacher, guide, and shepherd. He is the Spirit of Truth **[John 14:26]**. John also tells us that the anointing [Holy Spirit] teaches us everything. **[1ˢᵗ John 2:27]**.

Be sure to fervently engage these prayers by faith, get acquainted with the person of the Holy Spirit, and see your Christian life change to a higher level in Jesus Name!

PRAYER POINTS

1. *Father, thank you for sending your Holy Spirit to me.*

2. *O Lord, fill me afresh with the power of your spirit.*

3. *O Lord, heal every wounded part of my life through the power of the holy spirit.*

4. *O Lord, help me subdue every fleshly manifestation of sin in*

my body by the power of your spirit.

5. *O Lord, re-align my life and set me on the right track with the help of the holy spirit.*

6. *O Lord, let the fire of the Holy Spirit come afresh upon my life today.*

7. *O Lord, by the help of your spirit, let my life reflect the life of God.*

8. *O Lord, kindle in me the fire of love through the help of the holy spirit.*

9. *Holy Spirit, I want to be connected to you forever.*

10. *Holy Spirit, enrich me with Your gifts.*

11. *Dear Holy Spirit, quicken me and increase my desire for the things of heaven.*

12. *By Your rulership, sweet spirit of God, let the lust of the flesh in my life be crushed in Jesus' name.*

13. *Holy Spirit, increase daily in my life in Jesus' name.*

14. *Holy Spirit, my refiner, refine and purge my life.*

15. *Holy Spirit inflames and fires my heart now!*

16. *Dear Holy Spirit, lay Your hands upon me and quench every rebellion.*

17. *Holy Ghost fire, begin to burn away every self-centeredness in me.*

18. *Sweet Holy Spirit, breathe Your life-giving breath into my soul.*

19. Sweet Holy Spirit, make me ready to go wherever You send me in Jesus' name.

20. Holy Spirit, don't let me shut You out in Jesus' Name

21. Sweet Holy Spirit, never let me try to limit You to my capacity in Jesus name

22. Dear Holy Spirit, work freely in me and through.

23. Dear Holy Spirit, purify the channels of my life.

24. Let Your heart O Lord, consume my will.

25. Let the flame of the Holy Spirit blaze upon the altar of my heart.

26. Holy Spirit, let Your power flow into my veins.

27. Sweet Spirit Of God, let Your fire burn all that is not holy in my life in Jesus.

28. Holy Spirit, let Your fire generate power in my life.

29. Holy Spirit, impart to me with thoughts higher than my thought.

30. Holy Spirit, come as dew and refresh me.

31. Holy Spirit, guide me in the way of liberty.

32. Holy Spirit, blow upon me such that sin would no longer find a place in me.

33. Holy Spirit, where my love is cold, warm me up.

34. Dear holy spirit, continue to show your manifest presence in my life.

35. *Let my hand become the sword of fire to cut down evil trees in Jesus' Name.*

36. *Let the fire of the holy spirit destroy the spiritual rag of poverty in my life.*

37. *Every enemy of excellence in my life, be consumed by the power of the holy spirit in Jesus' name.*

38. *Dear Holy Spirit, let every past satanic achievement in my life be converted to my promotion.*

39. *Dear Holy Spirit, help me; let the shame of my enemies be multiplied greatly.*

40. *With the Power of the Holy Spirit at work in me, I barricade my life from every satanic opinion.*

41. *Dear Holy Spirit, thank you for causing me to ride above principalities and powers in the name of Jesus.*

42. *Father, thank you for the empowerment of the Holy Spirit.*

PRAYER FOR GROWTH IN THE SPIRIT

Every serious believer can grow spiritually. Just like every infant needs to keep growing to become an adult, every child of God needs to grow spiritually to be a mature Believer. There are two ways a Believer grows: Intense and ceaseless praying by the Word of God. These Holy Spirit-inspired prayer points below are a sure way to build spiritual muscles. As you pray them, give room for the Holy Spirit to work on you, in you, and through you.

In **[Luke 18:1],** Jesus taught us to pray always and not faint. These prayers will empower you to grow spiritually. It will boost your prayer life and, in turn, boost your spiritual development. It takes prayers to overcome temptations, and the more temptations you overcome, the more you grow spiritually.

Are you experiencing weakness in your Christian life? Are you lacking wisdom and direction? Prayer is the sure key to accessing anything in the kingdom.

PRAYER POINTS FOR SPIRITUAL GROWTH

1. *Father, we appreciate You for Your grace that we receive every day and the grace we have received to see this new day* **[Psalm 103:1-5].**

2. Father, we thank You for all the testimonies, intervention, divine supplies, and preservation we have experienced thus far **[Psalm 103:4-5]**.

3. Father, for all Your benefits – increase, promotion, the gift of life, we give You praise, Lord. **[Psalm 103:4-5]**.

4. We receive access into Your Presence by the Blood of Jesus **[Hebrews 10:19]**.

5. Father, we ask for the empowerment of the Holy Spirit as we pray today. We receive Your help Holy Spirit in Jesus' Name **[Romans 8:26]**.

6. Holy Ghost, I make demands on Your help today. As I pray, I connect Your power in Jesus' Name!

7. In the Name of Jesus, I shall not give up on this journey of faith.

8. My faith shall grow exponentially and unusually.

9. My faith shall produce results I have never seen before.

10. Father, as a people and as a Commission, we hand over everything to You.

11. Oh Lord, take absolute control of the month of March for my life, family, the Church, and the Nation in Jesus' Name **[2nd Timothy 1:12]**

12. In the Name of Jesus, Father establishes Your Throne in the Church and my life **[Daniel 4:17]**.

13. Father, in the Name of Jesus, in the month of March, let

Your counsel stand in the Church and my life. Do Your Pleasure Lord **[Isaiah 46:9-10]**.

14. *Father, thank You for Your allocation to us. In the Name of Jesus, I receive my provision for this Nation and the Church.*

15. *Oh Lord, let celestial officers be moved on assignment to make these provisions available now* **[1st Kings 4:7]**

16. *Father, in the Name of Jesus, we pray for the nations. We decree Your perfect will for the Nation at all levels.*

17. *Oh God, fight from Heaven; let the Hosts of Heaven fight against terrorism worldwide.*

18. *We decree the restoration of the glory of the Nations, let it be restored to its former glory, empower it Lord* **[Psalm 122:6; 1st Samuel 7:9-10]**

19. *Father, in the Name of Jesus, we speak to the economy – you are not permitted to fall anymore.*

20. *We decree the empowerment of the currency and economy of the Nation; rise back to where you used to be now!*

21. *Father, in the Name of Jesus, we declare mercy for the Oracle of God International Ministries.*

22. *By the mercy of God, not one person shall be consumed by stray arrows, strange bullets, or accidents.*

23. *We receive mercy for the Church in Jesus' Name.*

24. *We praise God for the favor, and the Lord is multiplying the Church.*

25. *We move higher in revival atmosphere, signs, and wonders in Jesus' Name* **[Lamentations 3:22].**

26. *Father, in the Name of Jesus, I come to You because Your Word says that if I delight myself in You, you will give me the desires of my heart.*

27. *I present my desires before You in Jesus' Name* **[Psalm 37:4].**

28. *Father, I receive an impartation of the Spirit of faith for all possibilities.*

29. O Lord, endue me with spiritual strength to be a doer of your Word.

30. Lord, establish me in my walk with you, like men see your good works in my life and glorify your name.

31. O Lord, establish me in your word; let your word bear fruits in my life.

32. God of peace, sanctify by your word, for your word is truth in Jesus' Name. Amen!

33. Father Lord, let my body, soul, and spirit be preserved blameless unto the coming of our Lord Jesus Christ, in the name of Jesus.

34. Let me be filled cause me to be filled with the knowledge of

your word as the waters cover the sea.

35. Oh Lord, endue me with the spirit of wisdom and spiritual understanding that I may comprehend hard truths in your word in the name of Jesus.

36. Lord, help me walk in your status, let people see Christ in me every day.

37. Father Lord, make me fruitful in every good work.

38. O Lord, baptize me with the spirit of supplication, increase my prayer life.

39. O Lord, strengthen me mightily in my inner man.

40. Lord, let me be filled with the power of your spirit in my walk

with you in the Name of Jesus!

41. *Father Lord, let the eyes of my understanding be enlightened in Jesus' Name. Amen!*

42. *Father Lord, let me be strengthened with might by His Spirit in the inner man in Jesus' Name. Amen!*

43. *Father Lord, let Christ dwell in my heart by faith, and let the love of Christ in me bear fruits.*

44. *Father Lord, let me be rooted and grounded in the love of Christ.*

45. *Lord, let me be filled with all the fullness of God.*

46. *God, help me comprehend the breadth, length, depth, and height of the love of Christ Jesus and cause me to walk in*

that love every day in Jesus' name.

47. Let the Word of the Lord have free course and be glorified in me in Jesus' Name. Amen!

48. O Lord of peace, give me peace in all areas of life.

49. Let utterance be given unto me to make known the mystery of the Gospel in Jesus' Name. Amen!

50. O Lord, perfect Your plan and purpose in me.

51. O Lord, make me your artistry, perfect for every good work.

52. O Lord, enrich me with supernatural wisdom in all utterance and knowledge.

53. Let the grace of the Lord Jesus Christ be with me.

54. Father Lord, inject into me your spiritual vitamins from your word [spiritual milk] that will make me spiritually healthy, in the name of Jesus.

55. Father Lord, inject into me spiritual vitamins that will boost my appetite to study Your word addictively, in the name of Jesus.

56. Father Lord, impart an undying spiritual hunger and thirst into me to pursue you like the dear pants after water in Jesus' Name.

57. Let God inject into me spiritual vitamins that will clear my vision and strengthen its clarity.

58. Lord God, I declare that I shall enjoy divine health in my

Christian walk in Jesus' Name. Amen!

59. *Lord God, impart tireless energy in my pursuit of divine assignment in the Name of Jesus!*

60. *Lord, feed me with the strong meat of your word for faster spiritual growth in Jesus' Name. Amen!*

61. *Lord God, boost my energy to run the race set before me to the end in the Name of Jesus Christ.*

62. *I receive the comforting anointing and power in the Holy Ghost in Jesus' Name. Amen!*

63. *Father, let the love of Christ flow from me to the rest of the*

world in the Name of Jesus Christ. Amen!

64. *I run into the name of the Lord, which is a strong tower, and I am safe in Jesus' Name. Amen!*

65. *Lord, thank you for empowering my spiritual life to scale higher height. In the Name of Jesus Christ.*

Other Books by
Apostle Stevie Okauru

The Christ we Eat
The Oracle decoding dream
The Oracle DIY Deliverance Kit
Effectual Fasting Kit
Miracle sermon note

Available on Amazon.com or Barnes & Nobles and other major books stores all over the world.

www.ingramcontent.com/pod-product-compliance
Lightning Source LLC
LaVergne TN
LVHW011830060526
838200LV00053B/3961